DATE DUE

DEC 3 0 2004			
APR - 8 2005			

DEMCO 38-296

AMERICAN
WAR LIBRARY

★ The American Revolution ★

PRIMARY SOURCES

Edited by David M. Haugen

LUCENT
BOOKS ®

THOMSON
—★—
GALE

San Diego • Detroit • New York • San Francisco • Cleveland • New Haven, Conn. • Waterville, Maine • London • Munich

Cover: "The Siege of Yorktown, 17 Octobre 1781"
by Augustine Coulder, (1789–1873)

For more information, contact
Lucent Books
27500 Drake Rd.
Farmington Hills, MI 48331-3535
Or you can visit our Internet site at http://www.gale.com

LIBRARY OF CONGRESS CATALOGING-IN-PUBLICATION DATA

Primary sources / [compiled] by David M. Haugen.
     p. cm. — (American war library. American Revolution series)
Summary: A collection of documents that includes the First Continental Congress's
"Declaration of Colonial Rights and Grievances," George Washington's "The Capture
of Boston," Charles Cornwallis's "Surrender," and much more.
Includes bibliographical references and index.
    ISBN 1-59018-238-3 (hardback : alk. paper)
  1. United States—History—Revolution, 1775–1783—Sources—Juvenile literature.
[1. United States—History—Revolution, 1775–1783—Sources.] I. Haugen, David M.,
1969– II. Series.
  E203 .P95 2003
  973.3—dc21
                                                2002010427

★ Contents ★

Foreword 5

Chapter 1: The Rift Between King and Colonies. 7

Chapter 2: The Shot Heard Round the World 30

Chapter 3: Year of Independence 53

Chapter 4: Campaigns 1776–1778 74

Chapter 5: On to Yorktown 99

Chronology of Events 119

Index 122

Picture Credits 127

About the Editor 128

A Nation Forged by War

The United States, like many nations, was forged and defined by war. Despite Benjamin Franklin's opinion that "There never was a good war or a bad peace," the United States owes its very existence to the War of Independence, one to which Franklin wholeheartedly subscribed. The country forged by war in 1776 was tempered and made stronger by the Civil War in the 1860s.

The Texas Revolution, the Mexican-American War, and the Spanish-American War expanded the country's borders and gave it overseas possessions. These wars made the United States a world power, but this status came with a price, as the nation became a key but reluctant player in both World War I and World War II.

Each successive war further defined the country's role on the world stage. Following World War II, U.S. foreign policy redefined itself to focus on the role of defender, not only of the freedom of its own citizens, but also of the freedom of people everywhere. During the cold war that followed World War II until the collapse of the Soviet Union, defending the world meant fighting communism. This goal, manifested in the Korean and Vietnam conflicts, proved elusive, and soured the American public on its achievability. As the United States emerged as the world's sole superpower, American foreign policy has been guided less by national interest and more on protecting international human rights. But as involvement in Somalia and Kosovo prove, this goal has been equally elusive.

As a result, the country's view of itself changed. Bolstered by victories in World Wars I and II, Americans first relished the role of protector. But, as war followed war in a seemingly endless procession, Americans began to doubt their leaders, their motives, and themselves. The Vietnam War especially caused people to question the validity of sending its young people to die in places where they were not particularly wanted and for people who did not seem especially grateful.

While the most obvious changes brought about by America's wars have been geopolitical in nature, many other aspects of society have been touched. War often does not bring about change directly, but acts instead like the catalyst in a chemical reaction, accelerating changes already in progress.

Some of these changes have been societal. The role of women in the United States had been slowly changing, but World War II put thousands into the workforce and into uniform. They might have gone back to being housewives after the war, but equality, once experienced, would not be forgotten.

Likewise, wars have accelerated technological change. The necessity for faster airplanes and a more destructive bomb led to the development of jet planes and nuclear energy. Artificial fibers developed for parachutes in the 1940s were used in the clothing of the 1950s.

Lucent Books' American War Library covers key wars in the development of the nation. Each war is covered in several volumes, to allow for more detail and context, and to provide volumes on often neglected subjects, such as the kamikazes of World War II, or weapons used in the Civil War. As with all Lucent Books, notes, annotated bibliographies, and appendixes such as glossaries give students a launching point for further research. In addition, sidebars and archival photographs enhance the text. Together, each volume in the American War Library will aid students in understanding how America's wars have shaped and changed its politics, economics, and society.

Chapter 1

The Rift Between King and Colonies

By the mid-1700s England's presence in North America was well established in Canada and in the thirteen colonies that ran along the eastern coast of America. For more than 150 years these lands—nearly three thousand miles from England—had enjoyed amicable and prosperous relations with their mother country. The New World provided Great Britain with raw materials (such as lumber) and food crops; in return, the colonies could purchase manufactured goods from England's factories. The relationship was mutually beneficial, and the colonists were content in their dependence on England.

During the 1760s, however, the English colonists in America began to reconsider the advantages of relying on a government so far from their own shores. The colonies were equipped with governing bodies of their own, and the men who filled them were able to quickly and practically address colonial concerns. Still, the

laws were handed down from the English Parliament and the English king, far removed from the realities of colonial life. When questionable laws pertaining to the colonies were passed, many colonists grumbled at the gulf that existed between the lawmakers and those who would be affected by their decisions. For example, when the French and Indian Wars ended in 1763, Parliament issued a decree that American colonists could not venture into newly acquired French territories west of the Appalachian Mountains. Many colonists believed they had a right to the land since they had shed blood to obtain it. They also felt that the colonies were overcrowded and that the virgin lands could provide breathing room. These facts were obvious to those in the colonies, but not so to Parliament in London.

The French and Indian Wars would, in fact, be the source for much of the colonial discontent over the next decade. Britain had run up a huge debt in defeating the

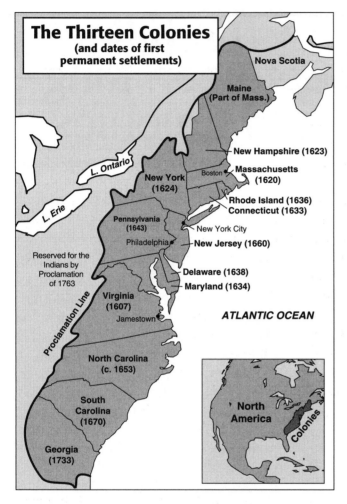

The Thirteen Colonies
(and dates of first permanent settlements)

Nova Scotia

Maine (Part of Mass.)

New Hampshire (1623)

New York (1624)

Boston

Massachusetts (1620)

Rhode Island (1636)
Connecticut (1633)

Pennsylvania (1643)

New York City

Philadelphia

New Jersey (1660)

Reserved for the Indians by Proclamation of 1763

Delaware (1638)

Maryland (1634)

Virginia (1607)

Jamestown

ATLANTIC OCEAN

North Carolina (c. 1653)

South Carolina (1670)

North America

Colonies

Georgia (1733)

L. Ontario

L. Erie

Proclamation Line

tax. The dissenters believed that Parliament had no right to impose taxes on the colonies since Americans had no representation in the body that enacted such measures. The common rallying cry of colonial opposition was "No taxation without representation." Furthermore, the angry colonists acknowledged that America already had governing bodies that determined fair taxation; they argued that if the Stamp Act remained in place, Parliament would find it easy to impose more taxes at its discretion.

Some members of Britain's Parliament were sympathetic to colonial complaints, and the Stamp Act was quickly repealed. But King George III and conservative members of Parliament wanted England's authority recognized. In 1766, as the Stamp Act was discarded, Parliament passed the Declaratory Act, which maintained the Crown's right to tax or otherwise manage its colonies, followed in 1767 by the Townshend Acts, which imposed taxes on imported goods and suspended some colonial governing bodies. In the colonies, the acts did not immediately stir controversy. After all, many colonists were loyal to the Crown and felt obliged to follow its laws. But some opponents of the taxes—most notably Samuel Adams, a member of the Massachusetts Assembly—spoke out bitterly against this infringement on colonial rights.

French and their Indian allies. Since the war took place in North America, Parliament decided the colonies should bear part of that financial burden as well.

To help raise the needed revenues, Parliament passed the Stamp Act in 1765. The Stamp Act levied a tax on some paper goods and placed a surcharge on specific legal documents. To the Crown's amazement, many colonists vocally opposed the

In Boston, Adams spearheaded a boycott of English goods that eventually gained support from merchants in New York and Philadelphia. Adams was also a member of the Sons of Liberty, a secret organization dedicated to maintaining colonial rights. The Sons of Liberty spread discontent among New England colonists. They also carried out terror raids on customs officials and other tax men who had to enforce Parliament's laws. In 1768 English troops under General Thomas Gage marched from New York to Boston to ensure the protection of the revenue collectors. Boston's citizens were not happy at the garrisoning of their city. Many treated the soldiers with derision. In 1770 the hostilities between the colonists and the soldiers came to a head. On March 5 a small detachment of British soldiers fired into a menacing crowd that had gathered in front of Boston's customs house. Five colonists were killed. The Sons of Liberty played up the tragedy as one of many heinous acts perpetrated by an uncaring Parliament.

In April 1770 Parliament repealed the Townshend Acts, primarily because British merchants were feeling the sting of the colonial boycott and complaining to Parliament. Then, in 1773, Parliament tried to save the ailing East India Company by exporting its teas to the colonies. However, the Tea Act of that year added a hidden tax to the East India tea. Despite the tax, the price of the tea was so cheap that Parliament thought the colonists would buy it. The colonists were not deceived. In Boston a group of disguised colonists boarded the East India ships at night and dumped the cargo of tea into the harbor. Lord North, the British prime minister at the time, believed this was a sign of rebellion. As part of a series of regulations to punish Boston, he had the harbor closed to all shipping. He also established a Quartering Act in 1774 that allowed for British troops to be put up in the homes of private citizens. These Intolerable Acts—as the collective regulations were called—were meant to force Boston into buying the East India tea.

Samuel Adams and the Sons of Liberty debate tactics to be used against the British.

Boston did not submit, and soon General Gage wrote to London to inform the Crown that he did not have enough troops to handle the huge mobs that gathered to protest the unjust laws. Other colonies were also taking Boston's side in levying grievances against Parliament. In September 1774 delegates from each colony met in Philadelphia to discuss a plan for bringing their complaints to the king in the hopes of avoiding further conflict. Although some delegates were in no mood for making concessions to England, the First Continental Congress adopted a petition that maintained the colonies' loyalty to the Crown but outlined the grievances they felt needed to be redressed by the king. When George III received the list of complaints, he was furious. He had already informed Parliament that the colonies were to be treated as if they were in rebellion. But before King George could make an official declaration of colonial treason, news reached him that colonial militia forces had fired on English troops outside of Boston. The Revolutionary War had begun.

James Otis argued that no government has the right to infringe on its citizens' God-given rights.

England Is Violating the Rights of Its Colonies

James Otis was a lawyer in Boston who believed that people had sovereign rights—including life, liberty, and property—which were granted by God. These rights are never abridged, even when the people appoint a government to rule over them for the common good. If a monarch or governing body infringes upon a citizen's God-given rights, then that citizen has the duty to demand a new government. In his well-known pamphlet Rights of the British Colonies Asserted and Proved, *Otis argues that by instituting taxes in the American colonies— ostensibly to pay for the costs of the late French and Indian Wars—the English government is overstepping its bounds of authority. In order to be taxed, Otis insists, the colonists must agree to the tax and they must have a voice in the government that imposes the tax. According to Otis, the colonists have no representative in England's Parliament, and therefore any tax levied by England is unwarranted. Otis's tract was written in 1765, a year after the passing of the Revenue Act (commonly known as the Sugar Act), which set taxes on goods such as sugar and coffee that entered colonial ports. His words warn that if the colonists accept these taxes, more will surely follow.*

The Colonists being men, have a right to be considered as equally entitled to all the rights of nature with the Europeans, and they are not to be restrained, in the exercise of any of these rights, but for the evident good of the whole community.

By being or becoming members of society, they have not renounced their natural liberty in any greater degree than other good citizens, and if it is taken from them without their consent, they are so far enslaved.

I cannot but observe here, that if the parliament have an equitable right to tax our trade, it is indisputable that they have as good an one to tax the lands, and every thing else. The taxing trade furnishes one reason why the other should not be taxed, or else the burdens of the province will be unequally born, upon a supposition that a tax on trade is not a tax on the whole. But take it either way, there is no foundation for the distinction some make in England between an internal and external tax on the colonies. By the first is meant a tax on trade, by the latter a tax on land, and the things on it. A tax on trade is either a tax of every man in the province, or it is not. If it is not a tax on the whole, it is unequal and unjust, that a heavy burden should be laid on the trade of the colonies, to maintain an army of soldiers, custom-house officers, and fleets of guard-ships; all which, the incomes of both trade and lands would not furnish means to support so lately as the last war, when all was at stake, and the colonies were reimbursed in part by parliament. How can it be supposed that all of a sudden the trade of the colonies alone can bear all this terrible burden. The late acquisitions in America, as glorious as they have been, and as beneficial as they are to Great-Britain, are only a security to these colonies against the ravages of the French and Indians. Our trade upon the whole is not, I believe, benefited by them one groat [a cheap silver coin]. All the time the French Islands were in our hands, the fine sugars, &c. were all shipped home. None as I have been informed were allowed to be brought to the colonies. They were too delicious a morsel for a North American palate. If it be said that a tax on the trade of the colonies is an equal and just tax on the whole of the inhabitants: What then becomes of the notable distinction between external and internal taxes? Why may not the parliament lay stamps, land taxes, establish tythes to the church of England, and so indefinitely. I know of no bounds.

James Otis, *Rights of the British Colonies Asserted and Proved*, 1765.

The Stamp Act Riots

Disappointed by the revenues of the Sugar Act, England's Parliament issued a tax upon paper

Angry business owners storm through town in protest of the Stamp Act.

goods in 1765. These goods, ranging from legal documents to playing cards, were to bear a stamp to show their taxable status. The so-called Stamp Act was tolerable to many Americans, but those whose business required paper—for example, lawyers and printers—were outraged. To counter the tax, many of these businessmen organized resistance. They boycotted taxable goods and even used threats and intimidation to scare off tax collectors. On August 14, 1765, the resistance

staged a riot in Boston. Governor Francis Bernard found himself powerless to quell the mob that eventually destroyed the city's stamp office and set out to capture the tax collector. In this letter, written to Lord Halifax and other members of Parliament, Bernard describes the events of the riot. King George and some members of Parliament took the news of this revolt as treason, yet by the end of the year, opposition in Parliament succeeded in repealing the Stamp Act.

I am extremely concerned, that I am obliged to give your Lordships the Relation that is to follow; as it will reflect disgrace upon this Province, and bring the Town of Boston under great difficulties. Two or three months ago, I thought that this People would have submitted to the Stamp Act without actual Opposition.

Murmurs indeed were continually heard, but they seemed to be such as would in time die away; But . . . an infamous weekly Paper, which is printed here, has swarmed with libells of the most atrocious kind. These have been urged with so much Vehemence and so industriously repeated, that I have considered them as preludes to Action. But I did not think, that it would have commenced so early, or be carried to such Lengths, as it has been.

Yesterday Morning at break of day was discovered hanging upon a Tree in a Street of the Town an Effigy, with inscriptions, shewing that it was intended to represent Mr. Oliver, the Secretary, who had lately accepted the Office of Stamp Distributor. Some of the Neighbours offered to take it down, but they were given to know, that would not be permitted. Many Gentlemen, especially some of the Council, treated it as a boyish sport, that did not deserve the Notice of the Governor and Council. But I did not think so however I contented myself with the Lt. Governor, as Chief Justice, directing the Sheriff to order his Officers to take down the Effigy; and I appointed a Council to meet in the Afternoon to consider what should be done, if the Sheriff's Officers were obstructed in removing the Effigy.

Before the Council met, the Sheriff reported, that his Officers had endeavoured to take down the Effigy: but could not do it without imminent danger of their lives. The Council met I represented this Transaction to them as the beginning in my Opinion, of much greater Commotions. I desired their Advice, what I should do upon this Occasion. A Majority of the Council spoke in form against doing anything but upon very different Principles: some said, that it was trifling Business, which, if let alone, would subside of itself, but, if taken notice of would become a serious Affair. Others said that it was a serious Affair already; that it was a preconcerted Business, in which the greatest Part of the Town was engaged; that we had no force to oppose to it, without a power to support the Opposition, would only inflame the People; and be a means of extending the mischief to persons not at present the

Objects of it. Tho' the Council were almost unanimous, in advising that nothing should be done, they were averse to having such advice entered upon the Council Book. But I insisted upon their giving me an Answer to my Question, and that it should be entered in the Book; when, after a long altercation, it was avoided by their advising me to order the Sheriff to assemble the Peace Officers and preserve the peace which I immediately ordered, being a matter of form rather than of real Significance.

It now grew dark when the Mob, which had been gathering all the Afternoon, came down to the Town House, bringing the Effigy with them, and knowing we were sitting in the Council Chamber, they gave three Huzzas by way of defiance, and passed on. From thence they went to a new Building, lately erected by Mr. Oliver to let out for Shops, and not quite finished: this they called the Stamp Office, and pulled it down to the Ground in five minutes. From thence they went to Mr. Oliver's House; before which they beheaded the Effigy; and broke all the Windows next the Street; then they carried the Effigy to Fort hill near Mr. Oliver's House, where they burnt the Effigy in a Bonfire made of the Timber they had pulled down from the Building. Mr. Oliver had removed his family from his House, and remained himself with a few friends, when the Mob returned to attack the House. Mr. Oliver was prevailed upon to retire, and his friends kept Possession of the House. The Mob finding the Doors barricaded, broke down the whole fence of the Garden towards fort hill, and coming on beat in all the doors and Windows of the Garden front, and entered the House, the Gentlemen there retiring. As soon as they had got Possession, they searched about for Mr. Oliver, declaring they would kill him; finding that he had left the House, a party set out to search two neighbouring Houses, in one of which Mr. Oliver was, but happily they were diverted from this pursuit by a Gentleman telling them, that Mr. Oliver was gone with the Governor to the Castle. Other wise he would certainly have been murdered. After 11 o'clock the Mob seeming to grow quiet, the (Lt. Governor) Chief Justice and the Sheriff ventured to go to Mr. Oliver's House to endeavour to perswade them to disperse. As soon as they began to speak, a Ringleader cried out, The Governor and the Sheriff! to your Arms, my boys! Presently after a volley of Stones followed, and the two Gentlemen narrowly escaped thro' favour of the Night, not without some bruises. I should have mentioned before, that I sent a written order to the Colonel of the Regiment of Militia to beat an Alarm; he answered, that it would signify nothing, for as soon as the drum was heard, the drummer would be knocked down, and the drum broke; he added, that probably all the drummers of the Regiment were in the Mob. Nothing more being to be done, The Mob were left to disperse at their own Time, which they did about 12 o'clock.

Governor Francis Bernard, letter to Lord Halifax, August 15, 1765.

England Affirms Its Authority over the Colonies

With the repeal of the Stamp Act, the marquis of Rockingham—the British prime minister at the time—had to quickly counter notions that Parliament had backed down to pressure from lawless mobs in America. Rockingham proposed the Declaratory Act of 1766 that reasserted the Crown's authority to manage its colonies in whatever way it deemed fit, even through the imposition of taxes. The act passed quietly through Parliament because most members who had opposed the Stamp Act interpreted the vague wording to imply that taxation was not included in the rightful legislation of the colonies. In America, the same confusion occurred, but a few careful readers recognized the ominous tone and the absolute authority that the document granted. When word spread, the colonists cried "tyranny."

Whereas several of the houses of representatives in his Majesty's colonies and plantations in America, have of Late, against law, claimed to themselves, or to the general assemblies of the same, the sole and exclusive right of imposing duties and taxes upon his Majesty's subjects in the said colonies and plantations; and have, in pursuance of such claim, passed certain votes, resolutions, and orders, derogatory to the legislative authority of parliament, and inconsistent with the dependency of the said colonies and plantations upon the crown of Great Britain: may it therefore please your most excellent Majesty, that it may be declared; and be it declared by the King's most excellent majesty, by and with the advice and consent of the lords spiritual and temporal, and commons, in this present parliament assembled, and by the authority of the same, That the said colonies and plantations in America have been, are, and of right ought to be, subordinate unto, and dependent upon the imperial crown and parliament of Great Britain; and that the King's majesty, by and with the advice and consent of the lords spiritual and temporal, and commons of Great Britain, in parliament assembled, had, hath, and of right ought to have, full power and authority to make laws and statutes of sufficient force and validity to bind the colonies and people of America, subjects of the crown of Great Britain, in all cases whatsoever.

II. And be it further declared and enacted by the authority aforesaid, That all resolutions, votes, orders, and proceedings, in any of the said colonies or plantations, whereby the power and authority of the parliament of Great Britain, to make laws and statutes as aforesaid, is denied, or drawn into question, are, and are hereby declared to be utterly null and void to all intents and purposes whatsoever.

Britain's Parliament, The Declaratory Act of 1766.

Eyewitness to the Boston Massacre

In 1767 England's finance minister, Charles Townshend, had several more acts passed through Parliament that would impose duties and other burdens on the colonies. In Boston, the new taxes were met with more protest. The fiery orator Samuel Adams called upon Boston merchants to boycott English goods. The businessmen agreed, and by 1769 New York and Philadelphia had joined the boycott. England demanded an end to the boycott and sent troops to Boston to keep control.

On March 5, 1770, outside the customs house where taxes for Boston harbor were assessed, a young colonist taunted a British soldier on sentry duty. The soldier reacted by clubbing the disrespectful colonist with the butt of his gun. Onlookers soon came to the colonist's defense, and a hostile mob formed. They insulted the sentry and pelted him with snowballs.

British captain Thomas Preston got word of the incident and assembled six soldiers and a corporal to reestablish order at the customs house. Arriving on the scene, Preston held the crowd at bay while the mood grew darker. Eventually one of the soldiers was knocked down, and getting to his feet he fired into the crowd, believing Preston had given the order. Other soldiers followed suit, and the mob scattered. Three colonists were dead in the street and another seven were wounded, two mortally. John Tudor was a Boston merchant who witnessed the whole affair and wrote the following account, which is surprisingly objective and lacking the inflammatory rhetoric of colonial propagandists such as Samuel Adams.

Fearing the massacre would provoke rebellion, the governor agreed to have Preston and his men tried for murder. But during the trial, many witnesses proved useful to the defense, and the jury believed the soldiers were unduly antagonized by the hostile crowd. Preston and four soldiers were acquitted; the other two were convicted of the lesser charge of manslaughter. Bostonians were enraged at the verdict, and tensions between England and its colonies became more strained.

This unhappy affair began by some boys and young fellows throwing snow balls at the sentry placed at the Customhouse door. On which 8 or 9 soldiers came to his assistance. Soon after a number of people collected, when the Captain commanded the soldiers to fire, which they did and 3 men were killed on the spot and several mortally wounded, one of whom died the next morning. The Captain soon drew off his soldiers up to the main guard, or the consequences might have been terrible, for on the guns firing the people were alarmed and set the bells a-ringing as if for fire, which drew multitudes to the place of action. Lieutenant Governor [Thomas] Hutchinson, who was commander-in-chief, was sent for and came to the council chamber, where some of the magistrates attended. The Governor desired the multitude about 10 o'clock to separate and go home peaceably and he would do all in his power that justice should be done, etc. The 29th regiment being then under arms on the south side of the Townhouse, but the people insisted that the soldiers should be ordered to their barracks first before they would separate, which being done the people separated about one o'clock. Captain Preston was taken up by a warrant given to the high Sheriff by Justice Dania and Tudor and came under examination about 2 o'clock and we sent him to jail soon after 3, having evidence sufficient to commit him on his ordering the soldiers to fire. So about 4 o'clock the town became quiet. The next forenoon the 8 soldiers that fired on the inhabitants were also sent to jail. Tuesday A.M. the inhabitants met at Faneuil Hall and after some pertinent speeches, chose a committee of 15 gentlemen to wait on the Lieutenant Governor in council to request the immediate removal of the troops. The message was in these words: That it is the unanimous opinion of this meeting, that the inhabitants and soldiery can no longer live together in safety; that nothing can rationally be expected to restore the peace of the town and prevent blood and carnage but the removal of the troops; and that we most fervently pray his honor that his power and influence may be exerted for their instant removal. His honor's reply was, "Gentlemen I am extremely sorry for the unhappy difference and especially of the last evening," and signifying that it was not in his power to remove the troops, &c., &c.

The above reply was not satisfactory to the inhabitants, as but one regiment should be removed to the castle barracks. In the afternoon the town adjourned to Dr. Sewill's meetinghouse, for Faneuil Hall was not large enough to hold the people, there being at least 3,000, some supposed near 4,000, when they chose a committee to wait on the Lieutenant Governor to let him and the council know that nothing less will satisfy the people, than a total and immediate removal of the troops out of the town. His honor laid before the council the vote of the town. The council thereon expressed themselves to be unanimously of opinion that it was absolutely necessary for his Majesty's service, the good order of the town, &c., that the troops should be immediately removed out of the town. His honor communicated this advice of the council to Colonel Dalrymple and desired he would order the troops down to Castle William. After the Colonel had seen the vote of the council he gave his word and honor to the town's committee that both the regiments should be removed without delay. The committee returned to the town meeting and Mr. [John] Hancock, chairman of the committee, read their report as above, which was received with a shout and clap of hands, which made the meetinghouse ring. So the meeting was dissolved and a great number of gentlemen appeared to watch the center of the town and the prison, which continued for 11 nights and all was quiet again, as the soldiers were moved off to the castle.

(Thursday) Agreeable to a general request of the inhabitants, were followed to the grave (for they were all buried in one) in succession the 4 bodies of Messrs. Samuel Gray, Samuel Maverick, James Caldwell and Crispus Attucks, the unhappy victims who fell in the bloody massacre. On this sorrowful occasion most of the shops and stores in town were shut, all the bells were ordered to toll a solemn peal in Boston, Charleston, Cambridge and Roxbury. The several hearses forming a junction in King Street, the theatre of that inhuman tragedy, proceeded from thence through the main street, lengthened by an immense concourse of people, so numerous as to be obliged to follow in ranks of 4 and 6 abreast and brought up by a long train of carriages. The sorrow visible in the countenances, together with the peculiar solemnity, surpasses description, it was supposed that the spectators and those that followed the corpses amounted to 5,000, some supposed 20,000. Note Captain Preston was tried for his life on the affair of the above October 24, 1770. The trial lasted 5 days, but the jury brought him in not guilty.

John Tudor, personal account of the Boston Massacre, 1770.

Report on the Boston Tea Party

Between 1767 and 1773 most of the Townshend Acts—the remaining taxes on goods imported to the colonies—had been repealed by the Crown. The tax on tea, however, was kept in place to remind colonists of Parliament's right to levy taxes as it saw fit.

In 1773 the East India Company—England's largest importer of tea—was facing bankruptcy and applied to Parliament for a special license to sell tea directly to the colonies, avoiding the duties usually levied in England.

The new prime minister, Lord North, agreed. Word of this deal angered most colonial tea merchants because the East India Company traded only with a few loyalist merchants in the colonies; the majority of merchants had to deal with other companies, which were not receiving the special exemption from England's duties. Thus, those who were favored by the East India Company could effectively undersell the other merchants.

On November 28 the Dartmouth, *the first of the East India ships, reached Boston harbor. Representatives of the angry colonists confronted the captain, Francis Rotch, and demanded he return to England without unloading his wares. Rotch complained that if he did not deliver his tea, he would be ruined financially. The Bostonians gave him twenty days to comply. On December 16, the eve of the deadline, the Boston lawyer and firebrand Samuel Adams convened a meeting attended by seven thousand colonists. Fed up with the delays, the crowd called for action. The meeting adjourned, and when night came, a gang of colonists—many dressed as Mohawk Indians or otherwise disguised—boarded the* Dartmouth *and two other East India ships that had arrived in port. With hatchets and crowbars, the mob broke open 342 tea chests and dumped 90,000 pounds of East India tea into Boston harbor. The Crown immediately shut down the port of Boston to all imports as punishment.*

On December 20 the Boston Gazette *published the following account of the Boston Tea Party. The* Gazette *subtly blames Lieutenant Governor Thomas Hutchinson—who was the acting governor at the time—for not sending the*

Bostonians disguised as Native Americans dump crates of tea from British merchant ships into Boston harbor.

ships back to England. The newspaper, like other presses with patriot sympathies, also refrained from mentioning any members of the mob by name.

On Tuesday last the body of the people of this and all the adjacent towns, and others from the distance of twenty miles, assembled at the old south meeting-house, to inquire the reason of the delay in sending the ship *Dartmouth,* with the East-India Tea back to London; and having found that the owner had not taken the necessary steps for that purpose, they enjoin'd him at his peril to demand of the collector of the customs a clearance for the ship, and appointed a committee of ten to see it performed; after which they adjourn'd to the Thursday following ten o'clock. They then met and being inform'd by Mr. Rotch, that a clearance was refus'd him, they enjoyn'd him immediately to enter a protest and apply to the governor for a pass port by the castle [getting permission from the navy to leave port], and adjourn'd again till three o'clock for the same day. At which time they again met and after waiting till near sunset, Mr. Rotch came in and inform'd them that he had accordingly enter'd his protest and waited on the governor for a pass, but his excellency told him he could not consistent with his duty grant it until his vessel was qualified. The people finding all their efforts to preserve the property of the East India company and return it safely to London, frustrated by the tea consignees, the collector of the customs and the governor of the province, DISSOLVED their meeting.—But, BEHOLD what followed! A number of brave & resolute men, determined to do all in their power to save their country from the ruin which their enemies had plotted, in less than four hours, emptied every chest of tea on board the three ships commanded by the captains Hall, Bruce, and Coffin, amounting to 342 chests, into the sea!! without the least damage done to the ships or any other property. The masters and owners are well pleas'd that their ships are thus clear'd and the people are almost universally congratulating each other on this happy event.

"Report on Boston Tea Party," *Boston Gazette*, December 20, 1773.

A Loyalist Reacts to the Tea Party

Ann Hulton was the sister of Henry Hulton, the customs commissioner for Boston between the years 1767 and 1776. In a letter to the wife of Adam Lightbody, a merchant in Liverpool, England, Hulton describes the effects of the Boston Tea Party upon the loyalists in Boston. Hulton was clearly a loyalist, and she had witnessed the continual insults and depredations waged against her brother and other customs house officials as they endeavored to carry out their jobs. She feared for the lives of the officials as they were forced to seek refuge in Castle William (where the British troops were garrisoned) and obliged to stay there for weeks after the events of December 16, 1773.

You will perhaps expect me to give you some Acct of the State of B——& late proceedings here but really the times are too bad & the Scenes too shocking for me to describe. I suppose you will have heard long before this arrives of the fate of the Tea—Whilst this was in suspence. The commissioners of the Customs & the Tea Consignees were obliged to seek refuge at the Castle [where the British troops were stationed]. My Brother happened to be there on a visit of a long engagement to Col. Lesley when those other Gentlemen came over. He continued there about twenty days, in the mean time visiting his own House (about 8 Miles from the Castle) several times. The Colonel & the Gentlemen of his Choir rendered the retreat as agreeable as possible by their polite Attention to every Refugee. After the destruction of the Tea. My Brother returned Home & the other Commissioners Left the Castle. The violent fury of the People having subsided a little. One would have thought before that all the Malice that Earth & Hell could raise were pointed against the Governor. Mr. Paxton (one of the Commissioners) & the Tea Consignees, two of whom are the Governors Sons, the others are Mr Clark a respecta[ble] Old Gentleman & his Sons, with two other Merchants Mr Haliwell another Commissioner & likewise of this Country was an object of their threats.

The Tea Consignees remain Still at the Castle. Six weeks since the Tea was destroyed, and there is no prospect of their ever returning & residing in Boston with Safety. This place, & all the Towns about entered into a written agreement not to afford them any Shelter or protection, so that they are not only banished from their families & homes, but their retreat is cut off, & their interest greatly injured by ruining their Trade.

It is indeed a severe case, & can hardly be credited, I think, that the Governors Sons should be treated as fugitives & outlaws in their own Country. One of them lately went from the Castle, & with his Wife to her Fathers House, a Gentleman at Plymouth 40 Miles from Boston They had no sooner arrived there, but the Bells tolled and the Town Assembling instantly went to the House, demanded that Mr. Hutchinson should depart immediately out of the Town. Colonel Watson his father in law, spoke to them, saying that it was so late at Night, & the Weather so severe, that Mr. H: & his wife could not without great inconvenience remove from his house that night, but promised them, they should go in the Morning by 9 o'Clock. The time came, and they were not gone, when the Town bells tolled again, & the people gathered about the house. Upon which the Young Couple set off in a great snow storm. & nobody knows since where they are.

But the most shocking cruelty was exercised a few Nights ago, upon a poor Old Man a Tidesman one Malcolm he is reckoned creasy, a quarrel was picked with him, he was afterward taken, & Tarred, & feathered. There's no Law that knows a punishment for the greatest Crimes beyond what this is, of cruel torture. And this instance exceeds any other before it he was stripped Stark naked, one of the severest cold nights this Winter, his body coverd all over with Tar, then with feathers, his arm dislocated in tearing off his cloaths, he was dragged in a Cart with thousands attending, some beating him with clubs & Knocking him out of the Cart, then in again. They gave him several severe whippings, at different parts of the Town. This Spectacle of horror & sportive cruelty was exhibited for about five hours. . . .

These few instances amongst many serve to shew the abject State of Government & the licentiousness & barbarism of the times. There's no Majestrate that dare or will act to suppress the outrages. No person is secure there are many Objects pointed at, at this time & when once marked out for Vengence, their ruin is certain.

The Judges have only a weeks time allowed them to consider, whether they will take the Salaries from the Crown or no. Governor Hutchinson is going to England as soon as the Season will permit.

We are under no apprehension at present on our own Acct but we can't look upon our Safety, secure for Long.

Ann Hulton, letter to Mrs. Adam Lightbody.

Instructions to the First Continental Congress

In response to the closing of Boston harbor and other perceived injustices, several colonies offered to send delegates to a Continental Congress to discuss the appropriate steps to take in protest of the Crown's actions. On May 27, 1774, the Virginia House of Burgesses—the colony's governing body—met in Williamsburg to select candidates to attend the First Continental Congress. They consulted with their constituents in the following weeks to gauge their support and seek their recommendations. The House then reconvened on August 1 and drafted the following set of instructions to their delegates. The orders convey the colony's ardent wish to settle current hostilities between England and America in an amicable manner. The Virginia burgesses even maintain their own loyalty to the Crown. But they insist that the acts of Britain's General Thomas Gage, who was then fortifying key positions in Boston and raiding colonial arsenals in case of uprising,
were illegal and should be met with resistance—armed resistance—if they did not cease.

The unhappy disputes between Great Britain and her American colonies, which began about the third year of the reign of his present majesty, and since continually increasing, have proceeded to lengths so dangerous and alarming as to excite just apprehensions, in the minds of his majesty's faithful subjects of this colony, that they are in danger of being deprived of their natural, ancient, constitutional and chartered rights, have compelled them to take the same into their most serious consideration; and being deprived of their usual and accustomed mode of making known their grievances, have appointed us their representatives to consider what is proper to be done in this dangerous crisis of American affairs. It being our opinion that the united wisdom of North America should be collected in a general congress of all the colonies, we have appointed the honorable Peyton Randolph, esquire, Richard Henry Lee, George Washington, Patrick Henry, Richard Bland, Benjamin Harrison, and Edmund Pendleton, esquires, deputies to represent this colony in the said congress, to be held at Philadelphia on the first Monday in September next.

And that they be the better informed of our sentiments, touching the conduct we wish them to observe on this important occasion, we desire they will express, in the first place, our faith and true allegiance to

Patrick Henry and Virginia legislators discuss armed resistance and reprisal.

the same rights and privileges as their fellow subjects possess in Britain; and therefore, that power assumed by the British parliament to bind America by their statutes, in all cases whatsoever, is unconstitutional, and the source of these unhappy differences.

The end of government would be defeated by the British parliament exercising a power over the lives, the property, and the liberty of the American subjects; who are not, and from their local circumstances cannot, be there represented. Of this nature we consider the several acts of parliament for raising a revenue in America, for extending the jurisdiction of the courts of admiralty, for seizing American subjects and transporting them to Britain to be tried for crimes committed in America, and the several late oppressive acts respecting the town of Boston, and province of the Massachusetts-Bay . . .

his majesty king George the third, our lawful and rightful sovereign; and that we are determined, with our lives and fortunes, to support him in the legal exercise of all his just rights and prerogatives; and however misrepresented, we sincerely approve of a constitutional connexion with Great Britain, and wish most ardently a return of that intercourse of affection and commercial connexion that formerly united both countries, which can only be affected by a removal of those causes of discontent which have of late unhappily divided us.

It cannot admit of a doubt but that British subjects in America, are entitled to

To obtain a redress of those grievances, without which the people of America can neither be safe, free, nor happy, they are willing to undergo the great inconvenience that will be derived to them from stopping all imports whatsoever from Great Britain, after the first day of November next, and also to cease exporting any commodity whatsoever, to the same place, after the 10th day of August, 1775. The earnest desire we have, to make as quick and full payment as possible, of our debts to Great Britain, and to avoid the heavy injury that would arise to this country from an earlier adoption of the non-exportation plan, after the people have already applied so much of their labor to the perfecting of the present crop, by which means they have been prevented from pursuing other methods of clothing and supporting their families, have rendered it necessary to restrain you in this article of non-exportation; but it is our desire that you cordially co-operate with our sister colonies, in general congress, in such other just and proper methods as they, or the majority, shall deem necessary for the accomplishment of these valuable ends.

The proclamation issued by general Gage, in the government of the province of the Massachusetts-Bay, declaring it treason for the inhabitants of that province to assemble themselves to consider of their grievances, and form associations for their common conduct on the occasion, and requiring the civil magistrates and officers to apprehend all such persons to be tried for their supposed offences, is the most alarming process that ever appeared in a British government; that the said general Gage hath thereby assumed and taken upon himself power denied by the constitution

to our legal sovereign; that he, not having condescended to disclose by what authority he exercises such extensive and unheard of powers, we are at a loss to determine whether he intends to justify himself as the representative of the king, or as the commander in chief of his majesty's forces in North America. If he considers himself as acting in the character of his majesty's representative, we would remind him, that the statute 25th Edward III, has expressed and defined all treasonable offences, and that the legislature of Great Britain hath declared that no offence shall be construed to be treason but such as is pointed out by that statute, and that this was done to take out of the hands of tyrannical kings, and of weak and wicked ministers, that deadly weapon which constructive treason had furnished them with, and which had drawn the blood of the best and honestest men in the kingdom, and that the king of Great Britain hath no right, by his proclamation, to subject his people to imprisonment, pains, and penalties.

That if the said general Gage conceives he is empowered to act in this manner, as the commander in chief of his majesty's forces in America, this odious and illegal proclamation must be considered as a plain and full declaration that this despotic viceroy will be bound by no law, nor regard the constitutional rights of his majesty's subjects, whenever they interfere with the plan he has formed for oppressing the good people of the Massachusetts-Bay; and therefore, that the executing, or attempting to execute such proclamation, will justify RESISTANCE and REPRISAL.

Virginia House of Burgesses, Instructions to the Continental Congress, August 1, 1774.

The Declaration of Colonial Rights and Grievances

The First Continental Congress met on September 5, 1774. By October 14 the delegates had adopted a series of resolutions that came to be known as the Declaration of Colonial Rights and Grievances. The representatives resolved that they had rights granted by the English constitution and other charters and agreements, as well as those inherent to all free individuals. These rights were, according to the Congress, be-

ing jeopardized by unlawful taxation and other acts perpetuated by a bullying Parliament. The colonists called upon the Crown to remove these impediments to the amicable relations between England and America in order to keep the allegiance of its colonial subjects. Until such time, the congressmen informed England that the colonies would boycott all English imports.

Whereas, since the close of the last war [the French and Indian War], the British parliament, claiming a power, of right, to bind the people of America by statutes in all cases whatsoever, hath, in some acts, expressly imposed taxes on them, and in others, under various presences, but in fact for the purpose of raising a revenue, hath imposed rates and duties payable in these colonies, established a board of commissioners, with unconstitutional powers, and extended the jurisdiction of courts of admiralty, not only for collecting the said duties, but for the trial of causes merely arising within the body of a county. . . .

And whereas, in the last session of parliament, three statutes were made; one entitled, "An act to discontinue, in such manner and for such time as are therein mentioned, the landing and discharging, lading, or shipping of goods, wares and merchandise, at the town, and within the harbour of Boston, in the province of Massachusetts-Bay in New En-

Congress posted a protest sign like this one to request that merchants boycott all English imports.

P H I L A D E L P H I A.

In CONGRESS, Thursday, September 22, 1774.

RESOLVED,

THAT the Congress request the Merchants and Others, in the several Colonies, not to send to Great Britain any Orders for Goods, and to direct the execution of all Orders already sent, to be delayed or suspended, until the sense of the Congress, on the means to be taken for the preservation of the Liberties of *America*, is made public.

An Extract from the Minutes,
CHARLES THOMSON, *Sec.*

Printed by *W.* and *T. BRADFORD.*

gland;" another entitled, "An act for the better regulating the government of the province of Massachusetts-Bay in New England;" and another entitled, "An act for the impartial administration of justice, in the cases of persons questioned for any act done by them in the execution of the law, or for the suppression of riots and tumults, in the province of the Massachusetts-Bay in New England;" and another statute was then made, "for making more effectual provision for the government of the province of Quebec, etc." All which statutes are impolitic, unjust, and cruel, as well as unconstitutional, and most dangerous and destructive of American rights.

And whereas, assemblies have been frequently dissolved, contrary to the rights of the people, when they attempted to deliberate on grievances; and their dutiful, humble, loyal, and reasonable petitions to the crown for redress, have been repeatedly treated with contempt, by his Majesty's ministers of state:

The good people of the several colonies of New-Hampshire, Massachusetts-Bay, Rhode Island and Providence Plantations, Connecticut, New-York, New Jersey, Pennsylvania, Newcastle, Kent, and Sussex on Delaware, Maryland, Virginia, North Carolina and South Carolina, justly alarmed at these arbitrary proceedings of parliament and administration, have severally elected, constituted, and appointed deputies to meet, and sit in general Congress, in the city of Philadelphia, in order to obtain such establishment, as that their

religion, laws, and liberties, may not be subverted:

Whereupon the deputies so appointed being now assembled, in a full and free representation of these colonies, taking into their most serious consideration, the best means of attaining the ends aforesaid, do, in the first place, as Englishmen, their ancestors in like cases have usually done, for asserting and vindicating their rights and liberties, declare,

That the inhabitants of the English colonies in North-America, by the immutable laws of nature, the principles of the English constitution, and the several charters or compacts, have the following RIGHTS:

Resolved, N.C.D.

1. That they are entitled to life, liberty and property: and they have never ceded to any foreign power whatever, a right to dispose of either without their consent.

2. That our ancestors, who first settled these colonies, were at the time of their emigration from the mother country, entitled to all the rights, liberties, and immunities of free and natural-born subjects, within the realm of England.

3. That by such emigration they by no means forfeited, surrendered, or lost any of those rights, but that they were, and their descendants now are, entitled to the exercise and enjoyment of all such of them, as their local and other circumstances enable them to exercise and enjoy.

4. That the foundation of English liberty, and of all free government, is a right

in the people to participate in their legislative council: and as the English colonists are not represented, and from their local and other circumstances, cannot properly be represented in the British parliament, they are entitled to a free and exclusive power of legislation in their several provincial legislatures, where their right of representation can alone be preserved, in all cases of taxation and internal polity, subject only to the negative of their sovereign, in such manner as has been heretofore used and accustomed. But, from the necessity of the case, and a regard to the mutual interest of both countries, we cheerfully consent to the operation of such acts of the British parliament, as are bona fide, restrained to the regulation of our external commerce, for the purpose of securing the commercial advantages of the whole empire to the mother country, and the commercial benefits of its respective members; excluding every idea of taxation internal or external, for raising a revenue on the subjects, in America, without their consent.

5. That the respective colonies are entitled to the common law of England, and more especially to the great and inestimable privilege of being tried by their peers of the vicinage, according to the course of that law.

6. That they are entitled to the benefit of such of the English statutes, as existed at the time of their colonization; and which they have, by experience, respectively found to be applicable to their several local and other circumstances.

7. That these, his Majesty's colonies, are likewise entitled to all the immunities and privileges granted and confirmed to them by royal charters, or secured by their several codes of provincial laws.

8. That they have a right peaceably to assemble, consider of their grievances, and petition the king; and that all prosecutions, prohibitory proclamations, and commitments for the same, are illegal.

9. That the keeping of a standing army in these colonies, in times of peace, without the consent of the legislature of that colony, in which such army is kept, is against law.

10. It is indispensably necessary to good government, and rendered essential by the English constitution, that the constituent branches of the legislature be independent of each other; that, therefore, the exercise of legislative power in several colonies, by a council appointed, during pleasure, by the crown, is unconstitutional, dangerous and destructive to the freedom of American legislation.

All and each of which the aforesaid deputies, in behalf of themselves, and their constituents, do claim, demand, and insist on, as their indubitable rights and liberties, which cannot be legally taken from them, altered or abridged by any power whatever, without their own consent, by their representatives in their several provincial legislature.

In the course of our inquiry, we find many infringements and violations of the foregoing rights, which, from an ardent desire, that harmony and mutual intercourse of affection and interest may be restored, we pass over for the present, and proceed to state such acts and measures as have been adopted since the last war, which demonstrate a system formed to enslave America.

[A list of English regulatory acts followed.]

To these grievous acts and measures, Americans cannot submit, but in hopes their fellow subjects in Great Britain will, on a revision of them, restore us to that state, in which both countries found happiness and prosperity, we have for the present, only resolved to pursue the following peaceable measures: 1. To enter into a non-importation, non-consumption, and non-exportation agreement or association. 2. To prepare an address to the people of Great Britain, and a memorial to the inhabitants of British America: and 3. To prepare a loyal address to his majesty, agreeable to resolutions already entered into.

First Continental Congress, Declaration and Resolves of the First Continental Congress, October 14, 1774.

Liberty or Death

When the First Continental Congress decided to institute a boycott of English goods until the king and the colonies could reconcile, not all Americans were content with this strategy. In March 1775 Patrick Henry, one of the delegates to the Continental Congress, rose before the Virginia House of Burgesses—*which had been officially dissolved by the Crown the previous year—to declare why he felt any concession to England would entail further subjugation of Americans. To Henry, the choice was obvious: true liberty or death.*

William Wirt was in attendance at the House of Burgesses and recorded the audience's reaction to Henry's stirring call to arms.

On Monday, the 20th of March, 1775, the convention of delegates, from the several counties and corporations of Virginia, met for the second time. This assembly was held in the old church in the town of Richmond. Mr. Henry was a member of that body also. The reader will bear in mind the tone of the instructions given by the convention of the preceding year to their deputies in Congress. He will remember

Patrick Henry rejects subjugation, proclaiming, "give me liberty, or give me death!"

that, while they recite with great feeling the series of grievances under which the colonies had labored, and insist with firmness on their constitutional rights, they give, nevertheless, the most explicit and solemn pledge of their faith and true allegiance to his Majesty King George III, and avow their determination to support him with their lives and fortunes, in the legal exercise of all his just rights and prerogatives. . . . These sentiments still influenced many of the leading members of the convention of 1775. They could not part with the fond hope that those peaceful days would again return which had shed so much light and warmth over the land; and the report of the king's gracious reception of the petition from Congress tended to cherish and foster that hope, and to render them averse to any means of violence.

But Mr. Henry saw things with a steadier eye and a deeper insight. His judgment was too solid to be duped by appearances; and his heart too firm and manly to be amused by false and flattering hopes. He had long since read the true character of the British court, and saw that no alternative remained for his country but abject submission or heroic resistance. It was not for a soul like Henry's to hesitate between these courses. He had offered upon the altar of liberty no divided heart. The gulf of war which yawned before him was indeed fiery and fearful; but he saw that the awful plunge was inevitable. . . .

He rose at this time with a majesty unusual to him in an exordium, and with all that self-possession by which he was so invariably distinguished. . . . "This," he said, "was no time for ceremony. The question before this house was one of awful moment to the country. For his own part, he considered it as nothing less than a question of freedom or slavery. And in proportion to the magnitude of the subject ought to be the freedom of the debate. It was only in this way that they could hope to arrive at truth, and fulfill the great responsibility which they held to God and their country. Should he keep back his opinions at such a time, through fear of giving offense, he should consider himself as guilty of treason toward his country, and of an act of disloyalty toward the majesty of heaven, which he revered above all earthly kings. . . .

"He had," he said, "but one lamp by which his feet were guided; and that was the lamp of experience. He knew of no way of judging by the past, he wished to know what there had been in the conduct of the British ministry for the last ten years, to justify those hopes with which gentlemen had been pleased to solace themselves and the house? Is it that insidious smile with which our petition has been lately received? Trust it not, sir; it will prove a snare to your feet. Suffer not yourselves to be betrayed with a kiss. Ask yourselves how this gracious reception of our petition comports with those warlike preparations which cover our waters and darken our land. Are fleets and armies necessary to a work of love and reconciliation? Have we shown ourselves so unwilling to be reconciled, that force must be called in to win back our love? Let us not deceive ourselves, sir. These are the implements of war and subjugation—the last arguments to which kings resort. . . .

"Let us not, I beseech you, sir [addressing the president of the House], deceive ourselves longer. . . . Our petitions have been slighted; our remonstrances have produced additional violence and insult; our supplications have been disregarded; and we have been spurned, with contempt, from the foot of the throne. In vain, after these things, may we indulge the fond hope of peace and reconciliation. There is no longer any room for hope. If we wish to be free—if we mean to preserve inviolate those inestimable privileges for which we have been so long contending— if we mean not basely to abandon the noble struggle in which we have been so long engaged, and which we have pledged ourselves never to abandon, until the glorious object of our contest shall be obtained— we must fight!—I repeat it, sir, we must fight!! An appeal to arms and to the God of hosts, is all that is left us!

"They tell us, sir," continued Mr. Henry, "that we are weak—unable to cope with so formidable an adversary. But when shall we be stronger. . . . Shall we gather strength by irresolution and inaction? Shall we acquire the means of effectual resistance by lying supinely on our backs, and hugging the delusive fantom of hope, until our enemies shall have bound us hand and foot? Sir, we

are not weak, if we make a proper use of these means which the God of nature hath placed in our power. Three millions of people armed in the holy cause of liberty and in such a country as that which we possess, are invincible by any force which our enemy can send against us. . . . There is no retreat but in submission and slavery! Our chains are forged. Their clanking may be heard on the plains of Boston! The war is inevitable—and let it come!! I repeat it, sir, let it come!!!

"It is vain, sir, to extenuate the matter. Gentlemen may cry, peace, peace—but there is no peace. The war is actually begun! The next gale that sweeps from the north will bring to our ears the clash of resounding arms! Our brethren are already in the field! Why stand we here idle? What is it that gentlemen wish? What would they have? Is life so dear, or peace so sweet, as to be purchased at the price of chains and slavery? Forbid it, Almighty God—I know not what course others may take; but as for me," cried he, with both his arms extended aloft, his brows knit, every feature marked with the resolute purpose of his soul, and his voice swelled to its boldest note of exclamation—"give me liberty, or give me death!"

He took his seat, No murmur of applause was heard. The effect was too deep. After the trance of a moment, several members started from their seats. The cry, "to arms!" seemed to quiver on every lip, and gleam from every eye.

William Wirt, *Sketches of the Life and Character of Patrick Henry.* Philadelphia: Claxton, 1818.

★ Chapter 2 ★

The Shot Heard Round the World

On the morning of April 19, 1775, a small group of colonial militiamen stood defiantly on the green of Lexington, Massachusetts—a small village outside Boston. The militia had been warned the previous night that British regulars were on their way to nearby Concord to seize some cannon and gunpowder stores in order to keep them from being used by the colonials if hostilities should break out in the Boston area. It was also known that the British detachment hoped to arrest John Hancock and Samuel Adams, two rebel leaders who were staying in Concord. The militia assembled in Lexington barred the path to the British objectives.

When the British column approached the small band of colonials in Lexington, the British commander ordered the militia to disperse. Seeing they were outnumbered, some colonials did begin to retire; others, however, stood firm. In the confusion a shot rang out from somewhere on the colonial side of the green. The British

soldiers returned fire, killing several militiamen and forcing the others to flee. The short battle was the first of the American Revolution. And the shot fired in defiance of injustice and tyranny was later commemorated by poet Henry Wadsworth Longfellow as "the shot heard round the world."

Although the British succeeded in driving off their foe at the Battle of Lexington, the mission to reach Concord would turn into a grievous military debacle. Even as Lexington's defenders fled, other militia units from nearby towns and even other colonies converged on the Lexington and Concord area. By the time the British marched to Concord, militia strength had grown considerably. The British commander tried to carry out his mission, but much of the colonial stores at Concord had been spirited away in the night, and Hancock and Adams had fled when word of the British advance reached them. At the North Bridge outside of

Concord, colonial militia barred further progress and actively engaged the British troops. The British force retired to Lexington. All along the route, militia hidden in roadside woods fired into the column of red uniforms. The harassment, the heat of the spring day, and the long march took its toll on the British regulars. Casualties mounted and exhaustion set in. When they stumbled on to Lexington green, nearly a third of the estimated six to eight hundred men in the British detachment were either wounded or too tired for duty. However, at Lexington the British met a relief column sent out from Boston. With their company, the survivors of Concord slowly wound their way back to the safety of the city.

The defeat at Lexington and Concord prompted King George III to declare the colonies in open rebellion. He sent more troops and badly needed generals to Boston. The city by this time had become an armed camp, surrounded on land by the colonial forces. General Thomas Gage, the military commander in Boston, was hopeful he could break the siege, but he was chastened by the colonial victory at Lexington and Concord. His newly arrived subordinates, William Howe, John Burgoyne, and Henry Clinton, were not so hesitant. On June 17 General Howe made a brash frontal assault against rebel positions near Bunker Hill, one of the many heights flanking Boston. The attack was unwise and costly, even though the British eventually carried the day. Having suffered more casualties in this their second engagement with the colonial militia, the British did not venture forth to attack from Boston again. The timidity and the

American revolutionaries won the Battle of Lexington and Concord that forced England to send additional troops to stop the rebellion.

two costly engagements forced General Gage out of command. King George III recalled Gage and placed Howe in command of the armies in New England.

Two days before the Battle of Bunker Hill, the Continental Congress met to appoint a supreme military commander for the colonial army (which was also officially created during these congressional sessions). The members chose George Washington, a Virginia planter, for the position. Washington had military experience, but many felt that he was too reserved and aloof for command. Washington, himself, insisted that others were more qualified to lead, yet—with Congress's nudging—he accepted the duty.

The Continental Congress named George Washington as the colonial army's military commander.

Washington took charge of the siege of Boston immediately. He kept the city cut off from supplies shipped overland. By the winter of 1775, Howe's army was feeling the effects of its imprisonment. Starvation and disease were rampant, and the British were forced to tear down buildings to get enough wood to keep fires burning. By the spring of 1776 Howe had had enough. He claimed he had always thought Boston was strategically unimportant, and he subsequently decided to evacuate the city. On March 4 the British army sailed to Halifax, Nova Scotia. Washington's ragtag army walked victoriously into Boston. The world was beginning to recognize the colonists—the "peasants" as General Burgoyne referred to them—as a formidable fighting force with a capable leader. Now the American patriots needed only to match their fighting prowess with a strong political bid for independence. In uniting the two, a new nation might free itself from its European shackles.

Paul Revere's Ride

In early 1775 General Thomas Gage, the new governor of Massachusetts and the commander of British forces in Boston, began securing colonial provision and munitions storehouses in Boston. Fearing an uprising, Gage even planned to go after powder stores in the communities around Boston. Unexpectedly, he received royal sanction for his scheme when Lord Dartmouth,

Silversmith Paul Revere (above) rides through the night (right) to warn of the approaching British troops.

the secretary of state for the colonies, sent him word that King George III had given his consent to use any means to restore the colonies to order.

Gage organized a special unit of handpicked regulars to proceed to nearby Concord, Massachusetts, to raid a colonial arsenal there and to pick up John Hancock and Samuel Adams, two patriot leaders who were staying in nearby Lexington. The mission was to be kept secret to avoid colonial interference, but the Sons of Liberty, a clandestine patriot spy network, found out about the plan and sought to warn the patriot militia at Lexington and Concord.

Paul Revere was a silversmith in Boston and a member of the Sons of Liberty. He and another agent, William Dawes, were given the task of carrying the news to the militia when the British made their move. Receiving a signal that the British would be ferried across Boston Bay—

thus indicating the route they would take to Lexington—Revere and Dawes rode through the night of April 18 to sound the alarm. Revere's account of his fateful ride is given below.

Revere and Dawes made it to Lexington and successfully delivered word to Hancock and Adams, giving them time to relocate to a safe house and prepare to flee the area. With the Lexington militia stirring, Revere and Dawes took the road to Concord. On the way, they met up with Samuel Prescott, a doctor from Concord who offered to join their cause. The three soon ran afoul of a British patrol. Revere was captured immediately, and Dawes was thrown from his horse after eluding the soldiers. Only Samuel Prescott avoided being caught or injured and carried word to Concord. By the time the British force from Boston arrived in Lexington the following morning, the patriot militia was ready for it.

I, Paul Revere, of Boston, in the colony of the Massachusetts Bay in New England; of lawful age, do testify and say; that I was sent for by Dr. Joseph Warren, of said Boston, on the evening of the 18th of April, about 10 o'clock; when he desired me, "to go to Lexington, and inform Mr. Samuel Adams, and the Hon. John Hancock Esq. that there was a number of soldiers, composed of light troops, and grenadiers, marching to the bottom of the common, where was a number of boats to receive them; it was supposed, that they were going to Lexington, by the way of Cambridge River, to take them, or go to Concord, to destroy the colony stores."

I proceeded immediately, and was put across Charles River and landed near Charlestown Battery; went in town, and there got a horse. While in Charlestown, I was informed by Richard Devens Esq. that he met that evening, after sunset, nine officers of the ministerial army [British regulars], mounted on good horses, and armed, going towards Concord.

I set off, it was then about 11 o'clock, the moon shone bright. I had got almost over Charlestown Common, towards Cambridge, when I saw two officers on horseback, standing under the shade of a tree, in a narrow part of the road. I was near enough to see their holsters and cockades. One of them started his horse towards me, the other up the road, as I supposed, to head me, should I escape the first. I turned my horses short about, and rode upon a full gallop for Mistick Road, he followed me about 300 yards, and finding he could not catch me, returned. I proceeded to Lexington, through Mistick, and alarmed Mr. Adams and Col. Hancock.

After I had been there about half an hour Mr. Daw[e]s arrived, who came from Boston, over the Neck.

We set off for Concord, and were overtaken by a young gentleman named Prescot, who belonged to Concord, and was going home. When we had got about half way from Lexington to Concord, the other two stopped at a house to awake the man, I kept along. When I had got about 200 yards ahead of them, I saw two officers as before. I called to my company to come up, saying here was two of them, (for I had told them what Mr. Devens told me, and of my being stopped). In an instant I saw four of them, who rode up to me with their pistols in their hands, said "G—d d—n you, stop. If you go an inch further, you are a dead man." Immediately Mr. Prescot came up. We attempted to get through them, but they kept before us, and swore if we did not turn in to that pasture, they would blow our brains out, (they had placed themselves opposite to a pair of bars, and had taken the bars down). They forced us in. When we had got in, Mr. Prescot said "Put on [Race away!]!" He took to the left, I to the right towards a wood at the bottom of the pasture, intending, when I gained that, to jump my horse and run afoot. Just as I reached it, out started six officers, seized my bridle, put their pistols to my breast, ordered me to dismount, which I did. One of them, who appeared to have the command there, and much of a gentleman, asked me where I came from; I told him. He asked what time I left it. I told him, he seemed surprised, said "Sir, may I crave your name?" I answered "My name is Revere." "What" said he, "Paul Revere"? I answered "Yes." The others abused much; but he told me not to be afraid, no one should hurt me. I told him they would miss their aim. He said they should not, they were only waiting for some deserters they expected down the road. I told him I knew better, I knew what they were after; that I had alarmed the country all the way up, that their boats were caught aground, and I should have 500 men there soon. One of them said they had 1500 coming; he seemed surprised and rode off into the road, and informed them who took me, they came down immediately on a full gallop. One of them (whom I since learned was Major Mitchel[1] of the 5th Reg.) clapped his pistol to my head, and said he was going to ask me some questions, and if I did not tell the truth, he would blow my brains out. I told him I esteemed myself a man of truth, that he had stopped me on the highway, and made me a prisoner, I knew not by what right; I would tell him the truth; I was not afraid. He then asked me the same questions that the other did, and many more, but was more particular; I gave him much the same answers. He then ordered me to mount my horse, they first searched me for pistols. When I was mounted, the Major took the reins out of

my hand, and said "By G—d Sir, you are not to ride with reins I assure you"; and gave them to an officer on my right, to lead me. He then ordered 4 men out of the bushes, and to mount their horses; they were country men which they had stopped who were going home; then ordered us to march. He said to me, "We are now going towards your friends, and if you attempt to run, or we are insulted, we will blow your brains out." When we had got into the road they formed a circle, and ordered the prisoners in the center, and to lead me in the front. We rode towards Lexington at a quick pace; they very often insulted me calling me rebel, etc., etc. After we had got about a mile, I was given to the sergeant to lead, he was ordered to take out his pistol, . . . and if I ran, to execute the major's sentence.

When we got within about half a mile of the Meeting House we heard a gun fired. The Major asked me what it was for, I told him to alarm the country; he ordered the four prisoners to dismount, they did, then one of the officers dismounted and cut the bridles and saddles off the horses, and drove them away, and told the men they might go about their business. I asked the Major to dismiss me, he said he would carry me, let the consequence be what it will. He then ordered us to march.

When we got within sight of the Meeting House, we heard a volley of guns fired, as I supposed at the tavern, as an alarm; the Major ordered us to halt, he asked me how far it was to Cambridge, and many more questions, which I answered. He then asked the sergeant, if his horse was tired, he said yes; he ordered him to take my horse. I dismounted, and the sergeant mounted my horse; they cut the bridle and saddle of the sergeant's horse, and rode off down the road. I then went to the house w[h]ere I left Messrs. Adams and Hancock, and told them what had happened; their friends advised them to go out of the way; I went with them, about two miles across road.

After resting myself, I set off with another man to go back to the tavern, to inquire the news; when we got there, we were told the troops were within two miles. We went into the tavern to get a trunk of papers belonging to Col. Hancock. Before we left the house, I saw the ministerial troops from the chamber window. We made haste, and had to pass through our militia, who were on a green behind the Meeting House, to the number as I supposed, about 50 or 60, I went through them; as I passed I heard the commanding officer speak to his men to this purpose; "Let the troops pass by, and don't molest them, without they begin first." I had to go across road; but had not got half gunshot off, when the ministerial troops appeared in sight, behind the Meeting House. They made a short halt, when one gun was fired. I heard the report, turned my head, and saw the smoke in front of the troops. They immediately gave a great shout, ran a few paces, and then the whole fired. I could first distinguish irregular firing, which I supposed was the advance guard, and then platoons; at this time I could not see our militia, for they were covered from me by a house at the bottom of the street. And further saith not.

Paul Revere, Memorandum on Events of April 18, 1775.

The Battles of Lexington and Concord

When the advance column of British regulars entered Lexington on the morning of April 19, 1775, they were met by a small assembly of seventy-seven colonial militia led by Captain John Parker. The colonial captain knew his men were not experienced enough to stand against the well-trained British troops, so after making a brief show of defiance, he ordered his militia to scatter without firing a shot. Some men chose to stand firm, but others calmly walked off the field. In the confusion, an unknown colonial fired into the British line that had formed on the edge of the green where Parker's men had assembled. The British returned fire into the retiring colonial militia, killing eight men. Parker's militia routed into the nearby woods.

The commander of the British force, Colonel Francis Smith, sent word back to Boston to have reinforcements sent up since he had not expected resistance. A relief column headed by Lord Percy was dispatched along with two cannon. By the time they reached Lexington, Smith's force had moved on to Concord. Along the way they met more colonial militia that had been converging on Lexington and Concord from surrounding villages. The militia fled toward Concord as the British advanced.

Upon reaching the town, Smith ordered a search for munitions and the securing of two bridges about a half-mile from the town center. A small detachment of about 80 men under Captain Walter Laurie was charged with holding the North Bridge. Laurie's small force was set upon by more than 400 militiamen who had been arriving continuously since the previous night. As at Lexington, a shot rang out and a confused firefight ensued. The British were driven from the bridge and fled into town. There, Colonel Smith was plagued by rumors that the countryside was swarming with rebels. Having waited in vain for Percy's relief column, he turned about and marched back to Lexington. Along the way, militiamen dogged his steps; small groups also laid in ambush along the route, sniping at the British column. By the time

the British reached Lexington, they had lost a considerable number of men. The soldiers had been on their mission for fifteen hours, and exhaustion and frustration were taking their toll. Lord Percy's relief column met Smith's group in Lexington. Together they made a forced march back to Boston, still harassed by militia hiding along the roadside. When they finally reached the safety of the city, Smith counted his losses. Around 240 soldiers had been killed or wounded in the debacle. American newspaper editors like Isaiah Thomas of the Massachusetts Spy *were quick to recount the events of the first great American victory. Thomas, a patriot propagandist, embellished many of the events, blaming the British for firing first despite, or perhaps ignorant of, the fact that unknown rebels had begun both conflicts.*

Colonial militia battle British troops as they arrive in Lexington on April 19, 1775.

The body of the troops . . . under the command of Lieutenant Colonel Smith, had crossed the river and landed at Phipp's Farm. They immediately, to the number of 1,000, proceeded to Lexington, about six miles below Concord, with great silence. A company of militia, of about eighty men, mustered near the meetinghouse; the troops came in sight of them just before sunrise. The militia, upon seeing the troops, began to disperse. The troops then set out upon the run, hallooing and huzzaing, and coming within a few rods of them the commanding officer accosted the militia, in words to this effect,

"Disperse, you damn'd rebels!—Damn you, disperse!"

Upon which the troops again huzzaed and immediately one or two officers discharged their pistols, which were instantaneously followed by the firing of four or five of the soldiers; and then there seemed to be a general discharge from the whole body. It is to be noticed they fired on our people as they were dispersing, agreeable to their command, and that we did not even return the fire. Eight of our men were killed and nine wounded. The troops then laughed, and damned the Yankees, and said they could not bear the smell of gunpowder.

A little after this the troops renewed their march to Concord, where, when they arrived, they divided into parties, and went directly to several places where the province stores were deposited. Each party was supposed to have a Tory pilot. One party went into the jailyard and spiked up and otherwise damaged two cannon, belonging to the province, and broke and set fire to the carriages. Then they entered a store and rolled out about a hundred barrels of flour, which they unheaded and emptied about forty into the river. At the same time others were entering houses and shops, and unheading barrels, chests, etc., the property of private persons. Some

took possession of the town house, to which they set fire, but was extinguished by our people without much hurt. Another party of the troops went and took possession of the North Bridge. About 150 provincials who mustered upon the alarm, coming toward the bridge, the troops fired upon them without ceremony and killed two on the spot! (Thus had the troops of Britain's king fired First at two separate times upon his loyal American subjects, and put a period to two lives before one gun was fired upon them.) Our people Then fired and obliged the troops to retreat, who were soon joined by their other parties, but finding they were still pursued the whole body retreated to Lexington, both provincials and troops firing as they went.

During this time an express from the troops was sent to General Gage, who thereupon sent out a reinforcement of about 1400 men, under the command of Earl Percy, with two fieldpieces [cannons]. Upon the arrival of this reinforcement at Lexington, just as the retreating party had got there, they made a stand, picked up their dead, and took all the carriages they could find and put their wounded thereon. Others of them, to their eternal disgrace be it spoken, were robbing and setting houses on fire, and discharging their cannon at the meetinghouse.

The enemy, having halted about an hour at Lexington, found it necessary to make a second retreat, carrying with them many of their dead and wounded. They continued their retreat from Lexington to

Charlestown with great precipitation. Our people continued their pursuit, firing till they got to Charlestown Neck (which they reached a little after sunset), over which the enemy passed, proceeded up Bunker's Hill, and the next day went into Boston, under the protection of the Somerset, man-of-war [naval warship] of sixty-four guns. . . .

Immediately upon the return of the troops to Boston, all communication to and from the town was stopped by General Gage. The provincials, who flew to the assistance of their distressed countrymen, are posted in Cambridge, Charlestown, Roxbury, Watertown, etc., and have placed a guard on Roxbury Neck, within gunshot of the enemy. Guards are also placed everywhere in view of the town, to observe the motions of the King's troops. The Council of War and the different Committees of Safety and Supplies sit at Cambridge, and the Provincial Congress at Watertown. The troops in Boston are fortifying the place on all sides, and a frigate of war is stationed at Cambridge River, and a sixty-four-gun ship between Boston and Charlestown.

Isaiah Thomas, editorial in *Massachusetts Spy*, May 3, 1775.

At Concord Bridge

Amos Barrett was a Concord minuteman—a member of the colonial militia that was reputed to be ready for action within a minute's notice. Barrett was one of around four hundred minutemen who fought at the North Bridge just outside of Concord. His brief account of the short firefight and pursuit of the British regulars through town reveals the same bravado exhibited by many who told of their exploits on April 19, 1775.

We at Concord heard they was a-coming. The Bell rung at 3 o'clock for an alarm. As I was then a Minuteman, I was soon in town and found my captain and the rest of my company at the post. It wasn't long

A minuteman receives word to meet at the town post and be ready to fight the British.

before there was other minute companies. One company, I believe, of minutemen was raised in almost every town to stand at a minute's warning. Before sunrise there was, I believe, 150 of us and more of all that was there. . . .

When we was on the hill by the bridge, there was about eighty or ninety British came to the bridge and there made a halt. After a while they begun to tear up the plank of the bridge. Major Buttrick said if we were all of his mind, he would drive them away from the bridge; they should not tear that up. We all said we would go. We then wasn't loaded; we were all ordered to load—and had strict orders not to fire till they fired first, then to fire as fast as we could. . . .

They stayed about ten minutes and then marched back, and we after them. After a while we found them a-marching back towards Boston. We was soon after them. When they got about a mile and a half to a road that comes from Bedford and Billerica, they was waylaid and a great many killed. When I got there, a great many lay dead and the road was bloody.

Amos Barrett, account of the Battle of Concord, ca. 1775.

Retreat to Boston

After the battles of Lexington and Concord, the British regiments under Colonel Francis Smith were obliged to retreat to Boston. Lord Percy was in charge of the relief force that aided Smith's men. Percy kept up an active defense as the main column of British regulars marched toward the city. Although Percy's men kept the colonial militia at bay, the rebels managed to harass the British all along the way.

Frederick McKenzie was a lieutenant in the Royal Welch Fusiliers, one of Percy's regiments. In his diary McKenzie recalls the tiring march and the menace of colonial snipers hidden in the surrounding woods and farmhouses. He even remembers the verbal taunts of the rebel pursuers who proclaimed their loyalty to patriot leader John Hancock over King George III.

During the whole of the march from Lexington, the Rebels kept an incessant irregular fire from all points on the column, which was more galling as our flanking parties, which at first were placed at sufficient distances to cover the march of it, were at last, from the different obstructions they occasionally met with, obliged to keep almost close to it. Our men had very few opportunities of getting good shots at the Rebels, as they hardly ever fired but under cover of some stone wall, from behind a tree, or out of a house; and the moment they had fired they lay down out of sight until they had loaded again, or the column had passed. In the road indeed in our rear, they were most numerous and came on pretty close, frequently calling out, "King Hancock forever".

Many of them were killed in the houses on the road side from whence they fired; in some, seven or eight men were destroyed. Some houses were forced open in which no person could be discovered, but when the column had passed, numbers sallied forth from some place in which they had lain concealed, fired at the rear guard, and augmented the numbers which followed us. If we had had time to set fire to those houses, many rebels must have perished in them, but as night drew on, Lord Percy thought it best to continue the march. Many houses were plundered by the soldiers, notwithstanding the efforts of the officers to prevent it. I have no doubt that this inflamed the Rebels, and made many of them follow us farther than they otherwise would have done. By all accounts some soldiers who stayed too long in the houses, were killed in the very act of plundering by those who lay concealed in them.

Frederick McKenzie, *Diary of Frederick McKenzie: Giving a Daily Narrative of his Military Service as an Officer in the Regiment of Royal Welch Fusiliers During the Years 1775–1781 in Massachusetts, Rhode Island and New York*, Vol. 1.

Proclaiming the Colonies in Rebellion

Just after the First Continental Congress sent its list of grievances to King George III, the English monarch informed Parliament that the colonies were to be considered in a state of rebellion. Americans knew nothing of this decision, and moderate members of the Continental Congress still hoped that England and its colonies could be reconciled. Their hopes were dashed, however, after the battles of Lexington and Concord. When news reached King George that Americans had fired on British troops, he issued the following

King George III declared that the colonies were in rebellion after receiving their list of grievances.

formal declaration of colonial rebellion on August 23, 1775. Word of the proclamation reached the colonies on October 31.

Whereas many of our subjects in divers parts of our Colonies and Plantations in North America, misled by dangerous and ill designing men, and forgetting the allegiance which they owe to the power that has protected and supported them; after various disorderly acts committed in disturbance of the publick peace, to the obstruction of lawful commerce, and to the oppression of our loyal subjects carrying on the same; have at length proceeded to open and avowed rebellion, by arraying themselves in a hostile manner, to withstand the execution of the law, and traitorously preparing, ordering and levying war against us: And whereas, there is reason to apprehend that such rebellion hath been much promoted and encouraged by the traitorous correspondence, counsels and comfort of divers wicked and desperate persons within this realm: To the end therefore, that none of our subjects may neglect or violate their duty through ignorance thereof, or through any doubt of the protection which the law will afford to their loyalty and zeal, we have thought fit, by and with the advice of our Privy Council, to issue our Royal Proclamation, hereby declaring, that not only all our Officers, civil and military, are obliged to exert their utmost endeavours to suppress such rebellion, and to bring the traitors to justice, but that all our subjects of this Realm, and the dominions thereunto belonging, are bound by law to be aiding and assisting in the suppression of such rebellion, and to disclose and make known all traitorous conspiracies and attempts against us, our crown and dignity; and we do accordingly strictly charge and command all our Officers, as well civil as military, and all others our obedient and loyal subjects, to use their utmost endeavours to withstand and suppress such rebellion, and to disclose and make known all treasons and traitorous conspiracies which they shall know to be against us, our crown and dignity; and for that purpose, that they transmit to one of our principal Secretaries of State, or other proper officer,

due and full information of all persons who shall be found carrying on correspondence with, or in any manner or degree aiding or abetting the persons now in open arms and rebellion against our Government, within any of our Colonies and Plantations in North America, in order to bring to condign punishment the authors, perpetrators, and abetters of such traitorous designs.

Given at our Court at St. James's the twenty-third day of August, one thousand seven hundred and seventy-five, in the fifteenth year of our reign.

God save the King.

King George III, A Proclamation by the King for Suppressing Rebellion and Sedition, August 23, 1775.

The Capture of Fort Ticonderoga

Although the colonial forces had won their first victories at Lexington and Concord, they were still badly in need of weapons—especially heavy cannon—if they were to match themselves against the British in Boston. Lieutenant Colonel Benedict Arnold of the Continental army believed the colonials could get what they needed from Fort Ticonderoga, a poorly manned outpost 150 miles from Boston on the shores of Lake Champlain. Arnold learned that Ethan Allen, another colonel who had been organizing a ragtag group of Vermont farmers into a militia unit, had the same idea and planned to undertake the mission immediately. Arnold asked Allen and his Green Mountain Boys to serve under his command, but Allen's men refused to

Ethan Allen and the Green Mountain Boys take control of Fort Ticonderoga.

obey anyone but their leader. Eventually Arnold and Allen made a joint assault upon the fort on May 10, 1775. The colonials surprised the British defenders and captured the fort's commander. They also seized one hundred cannon, which would be later used during the siege of Boston. Ethan Allen describes his part in the attack, as well as his own capture the next month while on a secret mission near Montreal, in his Narrative of Colonel Ethan Allen's Captivity, *published in 1779.*

Ever since I arrived at the state of manhood, and acquainted myself with the general history of mankind, I have felt a sincere passion for liberty. The history of nations doomed to perpetual slavery, in consequence of yielding up to tyrants their natural-born liberties, I read with a sort of philosophical horror; so that the first systematical and bloody attempt, at Lexington, to enslave America, thoroughly electrified my mind, and fully determined me to take part with my country. And, while I was wishing for an opportunity to signalize myself in its behalf, directions were privately sent to me from the then colony (now State) of Connecticut, to raise the Green Mountain Boys, and, if possible, with them to surprise and take the fortress of Ticonderoga. This enterprise I cheerfully undertook; and, after first guarding all the several passes that led thither, to cut off all intelligence between the garrison and the country, made a forced march from Bennington, and arrived at the lake opposite to Ticonderoga, on the evening of the ninth day of May, 1775, with two hundred and thirty valiant Green Mountain Boys; and it was with the utmost difficulty that I procured boats to cross the lake. However, I landed eighty-three men near the garrison, and sent the boats back for the rear guard, commanded by Colonel Seth Warner; but the day began to dawn, and I found myself under necessity to attack the fort before the rear could cross the lake; and, as it was viewed hazardous, I harangued the officers and soldiers in the manner following:

"Friends and fellow-soldiers, You have, for a number of years past been a scourge and terror to arbitrary power. Your valor has been famed abroad, and acknowledged, as appears by the advice and orders to me, from the General Assembly of Connecticut, to surprise and take the garrison now before us. I now propose to advance before you, and, in person, conduct you through the wicket-gate; for we must this morning either quit our pretensions to valor, or possess ourselves of this fortress in a few minutes; and, inasmuch as it is a desperate attempt, which none but the bravest of men dare undertake, I do not urge it on any contrary to his will. You that will undertake voluntarily, poise your firelocks [muskets]".

The men being, at this time, drawn up in three ranks, each poised his firelock. I ordered them to face to the right, and, at the head of the center-file, marched them immediately to the wicket-gate aforesaid, where I found a sentry posted, who instantly snapped his fusee at me; I ran immediately toward him, and he retreated through the covered way into the parade within the garrison, gave a halloo, and ran under a bomb-proof. My party, who followed me into the fort, I formed on the parade in such a manner as to face the two barracks which faced each other.

The garrison being asleep, except the sentries, we gave three huzzas which greatly surprised them. One of the sentries made a pass at one of my officers with a charged bayonet, and slightly wounded him. My first thought was to kill him with my sword; but, in an instant, I altered the design and fury of the blow to a slight cut on the side of the head, upon which he dropped his gun, and asked quarter [asked that he be spared], which I readily granted him, and demanded of him the place where the commanding officer kept. He showed me a pair of stairs in the front of a barrack, on the west part of the garrison, which led up to a second story in said barrack, to which I immediately repaired, and ordered the commander, Captain De la Place, to come forth instantly, or I would sacrifice the whole garrison; at which the Captain came immediately to the door, with his breeches in his hand. When I ordered him to deliver me the fort instantly, he asked me by what authority I demanded it. I answered him, "In the name of the great Jehovah, and the Continental Congress."

The authority of the Congress being very little known at that time, he began to speak again; but I interrupted him, and with my drawn sword over his head, again demanded an immediate surrender of the garrison; with which he then complied, and ordered his men to be forthwith paraded without arms, as he had given up the garrison.

Ethan Allen, *Narrative of Colonel Ethan Allen's Captivity, From the Time of his Being Taken by the British, near Montreal, on the 25th Day of September, in the Year 1775, to the Time of his Exchange, on the 6th Day of May, 1778.* Boston: Draper and Folsom, 1779.

The Battle of Bunker Hill

With the British forces trapped in Boston, the colonial militia seized the high ground north of the city and there planned to erect batteries of cannon to shell the city. The British governor and general, Thomas Gage, needed to be rid of this threat. In May 1775 reinforcements from Britain bolstered his forces to sixty-five hundred men. He also acquired three new generals: William Howe, Henry Clinton, and John Burgoyne. The four strategists met to decide how to secure the heights around Boston.

Colonel William Prescott directs the colonial militia to prepare for battle at Bunker Hill.

Howe, Clinton, and Burgoyne were contemptuous of Gage's performance up to then. Burgoyne refused to believe that the colonial "peasants" could stand up to English troops. It was clear to Gage that each of the newcomers was spoiling to prove his mettle. The plan the British generals devised entailed a frontal assault against the rebel positions.

For several days the colonial militia under the command of Colonel William Prescott had been fortifying two hills north of the city. On the night of June 16, Prescott decided to halt the work on Bunker Hill, believing it was less important than nearby Breed's Hill, which had a better command of northern Boston. All through the night, two thousand militiamen from several different New England colonies dug ditches and built palisades in preparation for the British attack.

Early on the morning of June 17, 1775, British ships anchored in the Charles River opened fire on the defenses on Breed's Hill. William Howe was given the task of leading the British infantry, but his advance was delayed until late in the afternoon because his troops needed to be ferried to their staging point. Around three o'clock, Howe's men—stretched out in battle lines—began their slow march up the hill. Companies of militiamen under Israel Putnam and Joseph Warren poured fire into the wave of oncoming British. Howe was forced to retreat. He sallied forth a second time and was likewise repulsed. By then, the colonials were running short of ammunition. They loaded their muskets with anything they could find, including scrap iron and nails. On Howe's third attempt, his infantry carried

The British begin their attack on Breed's Hill.

the hill. Several units of American militia had run out of ammunition and were reduced to throwing rocks. But despite their resolve, they lacked the one thing every British soldier possessed: a bayonet. Facing a line of glinting steel, the colonials fled the heights. The British had won a very costly victory: Of the 2,400 British soldiers engaged, 1,054—including 92 officers—had been shot and 226 of those had been killed.

An anonymous patriot militia leader wrote the following letter to a friend in England nine days after the battle. It was published in the London Morning Post and Daily Advertiser *about a month later. In the letter, the patriot describes the epic assault on Breed's Hill,* which would inappropriately be remembered in history books as the Battle of Bunker Hill.

Four thousand men commanded by General [Israel] Putnam, and led on by Dr. [Joseph] Warren, having prepared every thing for the operation as well as could be contrived or collected were stationed under a half unfinished breastwork and some palisades fixed in a hurry. When the enemy were landed, to the number of 2500, as we are since informed, being the light infantry and the grenadiers of the army with a complete train of artillery, howitzers and field pieces, drawn by 200 sailors, and commanded by the most gallant and experienced officers of the last war, they marched to engage 3000 provincials, arrayed in red worsted caps and blue great coats, with guns of different sizes, few of which had bayonets, ill-served artillery, but of invincible courage! The fire from the ships and artillery of the enemy was horrid and amazing; the first onset of the soldiers was bold and fierce, but they were received with equal courage; at length the 38th Regiment gave way, and the rest recoiled. The King's troops were commanded by General Howe, brother to that gallant Lord Howe to whose memory the province of Massachusetts Bay erected a statue. He marched with undaunted spirit at the head of his men; most of his followers were killed round his own person. The King's troops about this time got into much confusion and retreated, but were rallied by the reproaches of General Howe, and the activity of General Clinton who then joined the battle. The King's troops again made their push against Charlestown, which was then set on fire by them. Our right flank being then uncovered, two floating batteries coming in by the mill dam to take us in the rear, more troops coming from Boston, and our ammunition being almost expended, General Putnam ordered the troops on the left to retreat. The confusion was great for twenty minutes, but in less than half an hour we fell into complete order; the regulars were so mauled they durst not pursue us 200 yards, but almost the last shot they fired killed good Dr. Warren, who had dressed himself like Lord Falkland, in his wedding suit, and distinguished himself by unparalleled acts of bravery during the whole action, but particularly in covering the retreat, He was a man of great courage, universal learning and much humanity. It may well be said he is the greatest loss we have sustained. General Putnam, at the age of 60, was as active as the youngest officer in the field. We have lost 104 killed, and 306 wounded; a Lieutenant Colonel

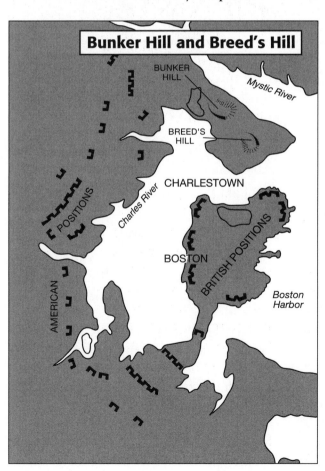

Bunker Hill and Breed's Hill

BUNKER HILL

Mystic River

BREED'S HILL

CHARLESTOWN

Charles River

AMERICAN POSITIONS

BOSTON

BRITISH POSITIONS

Boston Harbor

and 30 men are prisoners, and we anxiously wait their fate. We lost before the action began 18 men by the fire of the ships and the battery from Boston, burying them before the assault. The number of the King's troops killed and wounded are three times our loss. A sailor belonging to one of the transports, who was busy with many of his companions in rifling the dead, and who has since deserted, assured me the ground was covered with officers. The cannonading was dreadful. The King's troops began firing at a great distance, being scarce of ammunition deferred our fire. It was impossible to send troops from Roxburgh, because we expected an attack there, or at Dorchester neck. I am well informed many of the old English officers are since dead.

A Leader of the Provincial Forces, letter regarding the Battle of Bunker Hill, June 26, 1775.

An Assessment of Bunker Hill

General William Howe personally led the British forces on their three charges against the fortified rebel positions on Breed's Hill. After the second attempt, many of his officers begged him not to try another frontal assault. The hillside was already littered with the dead and injured. But Howe was headstrong and, supplied with reinforcements, he carried the hill on the third charge.

After the costly battle, Howe became more sober about his losses. In this letter to a confidant, Howe—though never blaming himself for the Pyrrhic victory—acknowledges how costly the attack was and how few troops were now left to defend Boston. Howe then recognizes that the hit-and-run tactics employed by the patriot armies will eventually dwindle the British forces until they can no longer maintain control of the colonies or the war.

I freely confess to you, when I look to the consequences of it, in the loss of so many brave officers, I do it with horror. The success is too dearly bought. Our killed, serjeants and rank and file, about 160; 300 wounded and in hospital, with as many more incapable of present duty. The Rebels left near 100 killed and 30 wounded, but I have this morning learnt from a deserter from them that they had 300 killed and a great number wounded.

We took five pieces of cannon, and their numbers are said to have been near 6,000, but I do not suppose they had more than between 4 and 5,000 engaged. . .

Entre nous [between us], I have heard a bird sing that we can do no more this campaign than endeavour to preserve the town of Boston, which it is supposed the Rebels mean to destroy by fire or sword or both—and it is my opinion, with the strength we shall have collected here upon the arrival of the 4 battalions last from Ireland. . ., that we must not risk endangering the loss of Boston—tho' should anything offer in our favour, I should hope we may not let pass the opportunity.

The intentions of these wretches are to fortify every post in our way; wait to be attacked at every one, having their rear secure, destroying as many of us as they can before they set out to their next strong situation, and, in this defensive mode (the whole country coming into them upon every action), they must in the end get the better of our small numbers. We can not, (as the General [Thomas Gage] tells us) muster more now than 3,400 rank and file for duty, including the Marines, and the three last regiments from Ireland.

William Howe, Assessment of the Battle of Bunker Hill, 1775, in Sir John Fortescue, ed., *The Correspondence of King George the Third, from 1760 to December 1783.* 6 vols. London: Macmillan and Company, 1927–1928. Courtesy of Librarian, Windsor Castle.

Writing to his wife Martha (pictured) George Washington confides his uneasiness about leading the Continental army.

Farewell to Martha

On June 15, 1775, two days before the Battle of Bunker Hill, the Second Continental Congress made a momentous decision that would have a decidedly favorable impact on the American struggle for independence. The body of congressmen appointed George Washington to lead the as-yet-to-be-raised Continental army. Washington was a Virginia planter whose selection to the post was not based on his military prowess (though he had been a commander in the French and Indian Wars) but on his southern heritage. Many northern congressmen believed that the appointment of a gentleman from the South would help ensure that the southern colonies would support the war against England— which at that point was chiefly raging in and around Boston.

Washington accepted the position reluctantly. He felt that there were other veterans with more experience who could handle the army with greater

confidence. But Congress was adamant in its choice, and Washington answered his calling. In this letter to his wife, Martha (known affectionately as Patsy), the new general of the Continental army writes of his anxieties in taking command. Bidding her farewell, Washington informs his wife that he must rush to Boston immediately to assume his post. He also mentions that he has drafted a will in case he should meet his end in the war.

My Dearest: I am now set down to write to you on a subject, which fills me with inexpressible concern, and this concern is greatly aggravated and increased, when I reflect upon the uneasiness I know it will give you. It has been determined in Congress, that the whole army raised for the defense of the American cause shall be put under my care, and that it is necessary for me to proceed immediately to Boston to take upon me the command of it.

You may believe me, my dear Patsy, when I assure you, in the most solemn manner, that, so far from seeking this appointment, I have used every endeavor in my power to avoid it, not only from my unwillingness to part with you and the family, but from a consciousness of its being a trust too great for my capacity, and that I should enjoy more real happiness in one month with you at home, than I have the most distant prospect of finding abroad, if my stay were to be seven times seven years. But as it has been a kind of destiny that has thrown me upon this service, I shall hope that my undertaking it is designed to answer some good purpose. You might, and I suppose did perceive, from the tenor of my letters, that I was apprehensive I could not avoid this appointment, as I did not pretend to intimate when I should return. That was the case. It was utterly out of my power to refuse this appointment, without exposing my character to such censures, as would have reflected dishonor upon myself, and given pain to my friends. This, I am sure, could not, and ought not, to be pleasing to you, and must have lessened me considerably in my own esteem. I shall rely, therefore, confidently on that Providence, which has heretofore preserved and been bountiful to me, not doubting but that I shall return safe to you in the fall. I shall feel no pain from the toil or the danger of the campaign; my unhappiness will flow from the uneasiness I know you will feel from being left alone. I therefore beg, that you will summon your whole fortitude, and pass your time as agreeably as possible. Nothing will give me so much sincere satisfaction as to hear this, and to hear it from your own pen. My earnest and ardent desire is, that you would pursue any plan that is most likely to produce content, and a tolerable degree of tranquility; as it must add greatly to my uneasy feelings to hear, that you are dissatisfied or complaining at what I really could not avoid.

As life is always uncertain, and common prudence dictates to every man the necessity of settling his temporal concerns, while it is in his power, and while the mind is calm and undisturbed, I have, since I came to this place (for I had not time to do it before I left home) got Colonel Pendleton to draft a will for me, by the directions I gave him, which will I now enclose. The provision made for you in case of my death will, I hope, be agreeable.

I shall add nothing more, as I have several letters to write, but to desire that you will remember me to your friends, and to assure you that I am, with the most unfeigned regard, my dear Patsy, your affectionate, &c.

George Washington, Farewell letter to Martha Washington, June 18, 1775, in John C. Fitzpatrick, ed., *The Writings of George Washington, from the Original Manuscript Sources, 1745–1799.* 39 vols. Washington, D.C.: United States Government Printing Office, 1931–1944.

The Capture of Boston

When George Washington officially assumed command of the Continental army on July 4, 1775, his first important task was to lay siege to Boston. After their costly victory at Bunker Hill, the British remained in and around the city, anticipating orders and awaiting reinforcements from England. Observing the hesitancy of the British generals to venture forth, Washington sent his army to secure Dorchester Heights, from which they would have a commanding view of Boston and could bombard the city with ease. Washington laid siege to Boston for nine months, constantly worried that his militia

---

Patience and strategy served George Washington well in the siege on Boston.

units—which made up the bulk of his forces and often disbanded without notice to return to their farms—would desert him at the exact moment the British would counterattack. Washington's luck held out, though. The British were frustrated at their own immobility. General William Howe complained that no orders or help had come from England for months. Furthermore, Washington's bombardment was taking its toll on British morale.

On June 27, 1776, with the help of the British fleet in Boston harbor, the British troops, along with thousands of Tories—colonists loyal to the English king—sailed out of Boston and headed for Halifax, Nova Scotia. In the following letter to John Hancock, the president of the Continental Congress, General Washington expresses his satisfaction that the campaign was successful. He even informs Hancock that his own manor house in Boston was untouched by the colonial siege.

It is with the greatest pleasure I inform you that on Sunday last, the instant, about nine o'clock in the forenoon, the ministerial army evacuated the town of Boston, and that the forces of the United Colonies are now in actual possession thereof. I beg leave to congratulate you, Sir, and the honorable Congress, on this happy event, and particularly as it was effected without endangering the lives and property of the remaining unhappy inhabitants.

I have great reason to imagine their flight was precipitated by the appearance of a work, which I had ordered to be thrown up last Saturday night on an eminence at

Dorchester, which lies nearest to Boston Neck, called Nook's Hill. The town, although it has suffered greatly, is not in so bad a state as I expected to find it; and I have a particular pleasure in being able to inform you, Sir, that your house has received no damage worth mentioning. Your furniture is in tolerable order, and the family pictures are all left entire and untouched. Captain Cazneau takes charge of the whole, until he shall receive further orders from you.

As soon as the ministerial troops had quitted the town, I ordered a thousand men (who had the smallpox), under command of General [Israel] Putnam, to take possession of the heights, which I shall endeavor to fortify in such a manner, as to prevent their return, should they attempt it. But, as they are still in the harbor, I thought it not prudent to march off with the main body of the army, until I should be fully satisfied they had quitted the coast. I have, therefore, only detached five regiments, besides the rifle battalion, to New York, and shall keep the remainder here till all suspicion of their return ceases.

The situation in which I found their works evidently discovered, that their retreat was made with the greatest precipitation. They have left their barracks and other works of wood at Bunker's Hill all standing, and have destroyed but a small part of their lines. They have also left a number of fine pieces of cannon, which they first spiked up, also a very large iron mortar; and, (as I am informed,) they have thrown another over the end of your wharf. I have employed proper persons to drill the cannon, and doubt not I shall save the most of them. I am not yet able to procure an exact list of all the stores they have left. As soon as it can be done, I shall take care to transmit it to you. From an estimate of what the quartermaster-general has already discovered, the amount will be twenty-five or thirty thousand pounds.

Part of the powder mentioned in yours of the 6th instant has already arrived. The remainder I have ordered to be stopped on the road, as we shall have no occasion for it here. The letter to General [John] Thomas, I immediately sent to him. He desired leave, for three or four days, to settle some of his private affairs; after which, he will set out for his command in Canada. I am happy that my conduct in intercepting Lord Drummond's letter is approved of by Congress. I have the honor to be, &c.

George Washington, Report to John Hancock on the capture of Boston, 1776, in John C. Fitzpatrick, ed., *The Writings of George Washington, from the Original Manuscript Sources, 1745–1799.* 39 vols. Washington, D.C.: United States Government Printing Office, 1931–1944.

Chapter 3

Year of Independence

When the First Continental Congress met in 1774, its agenda was to convince the English Crown that the colonies had just complaints regarding parliamentary laws. The colonists were still hoping to redress these matters amicably with England. By 1776, when the Second Continental Congress convened, there was no such sentiment. The tensions between England and its colonies had erupted into war, and reconciliation was no longer an option—regardless of whether a third of America's colonists still considered themselves to be loyal English subjects. The discussions of the Second Continental Congress focused on declaring American independence.

Although some members of the Continental Congress feared that the colonies were not financially or militarily strong enough to stand on their own, the majority of the convention was in favor of proclaiming America a sovereign nation. Several astute congressmen such as Richard

Henry Lee acknowledged that, as an independent country, America could begin diplomatic relations with other foreign powers and perhaps entice them to help support the new nation's struggle against England. To help convince other nations of the righteousness of America's intentions, the Congress voted to draft a document that would spell out the reasons behind America's bid for independence and the ideals that would serve as the country's philosophical foundation. A special committee was selected to contribute to the creation of this declaration, but only one man was chosen to write it.

Thomas Jefferson was a thirty-three-year-old scholar from Virginia who served on this committee. Jefferson was not a vocal member of the Congress, but other delegates respected his thoughts. In 1774 he had written *A Summary View of Rights of British America*, which many members believed captured the essence of America's complaints against George III. Those who

The Continental Congress met in this building to ratify the Declaration of Independence.

had read this pamphlet acknowledged that it was both well argued and well written. For these reasons, the select committee members nominated Jefferson to draft the document proclaiming American independence. Jefferson was a modest man, and at first he begged off the assignment. He asserted that John Adams, the cousin of Samuel Adams, should carry out this important task. Adams assured Jefferson that the right man had been chosen, particularly since Adams had persuaded the other members to nominate Jefferson. Jefferson relented, saying, "Well, if you are decided, I will do as well as I can."

In June 1776 he began drafting the document. Although Jefferson wrote what he believed were the common ideals shared by the Congress, he infused his own beliefs on personal liberty into the declaration. He also borrowed from *A Summary View of Rights* as well as the Virginia constitution, which he also authored. In the end, the Declaration of Independence mirrored Jefferson's previous lists of grievances against the king but also stressed fundamental notions that "all men are created equal" and entitled to specific "unalienable rights," including "life, liberty and the pursuit of happiness." The final draft was submitted to the Continental Congress for approval. Many of Jefferson's words were changed or deleted as members pored over the text. Most significantly, Jefferson's condemnation of slavery was excised so as not to offend slaveholders in the colonies.

On July 1 the final document was read before Congress, and the delegates took up the issue of voting on declaring American independence. A few dissenting voices were heard, but John Adams made a reasoned speech that persuaded many members to vote for independence. Still, the final tally was delayed until the next day. By then, word had come from George Washington that the British army seemed poised to attack colonial positions around New York. The news swayed undecided delegates. On July 2 the vote was unanimously in favor of making the former British colonies into a union of free and independent states.

Common Sense

By 1776 the first shots of the Revolution had been fired, but many colonists were still unsure whether war was the correct manner in which to resolve their differences with England. Thomas Paine was not one of those harboring doubts.

Though the son of an English Quaker, Paine was not hesitant in supporting armed resistance when colonial liberties were threatened. In his widely read pamphlet Common Sense—*published anonymously in January 1776—Paine insisted that America should be independent from England. This independence should not be motivated by mere dislike for the remaining pecuniary taxes levied by England, but rather for the tyrannical and martial manner in which the colonies have been kept enslaved. Paine even argued that independence would be in the best*

Thomas Paine believed that threats against liberty warranted armed resistance.

interests of both America and England since Britain's chief interest in the colonies was commercial and America had no better trading partner than England. In the following extract from Common Sense, *Paine concludes by imploring all Americans—patriots (Whigs), loyalists (Tories), and the undecided—to pull together and seize the opportunity to build a new, independent nation founded on the principles of freedom.*

The taking up arms, merely to enforce the repeal of a pecuniary law seems as unwarrantable by the divine law, and as repugnant to human feelings, as the taking up arms to enforce the obedience thereto. The object, on either side, does not justify the means; for the lives of men are too valuable, to be cast away on such trifles. It is the violence which is done and threatened to our persons; the destruction of our property by an armed force; the invasion of our country by fire and sword, which conscientiously qualifies the use of arms: And the instant, in which such a mode of defense became necessary, all subjection to Britain ought to have ceased; and the independency of America, should have been considered, as dating its era from, and published, by the first musket that was fired against her. This line is a line of consistency; neither drawn by caprice, nor extended by ambition; but produced by a chain of events, of which the colonies were not the authors.

I shall conclude these remarks, with the following timely and well intended hint. We ought to reflect that there are three different ways, by which an independency may hereafter be effected; and that one of those three, will one day or other, be the fate of America, viz. By the legal voice of the people in Congress; by a military power; or by a mob. It may not always happen that our soldiers are citizens, and the multitude a body of reasonable men; virtue, as I have already remarked, is not hereditary, neither is it perpetual. Should an independency be brought about by the first of those means, we have every opportunity and every encouragement before us, to form the noblest purest constitution on the face of the earth. We have it in our power to begin the world over again. A situation, similar to the present, has not happened since the days of Noah until now. The birthday of a new world is at hand, and a race of men, perhaps as numerous as all Europe contains, are to receive their portion of freedom from the event of a few months. The reflection is awful and in this point of view, how trifling, how ridiculous, do the little paltry cavilings, of a few weak or interested men appear, when weighed against the business of a world. . . .

In short, independence is the only bond that can tie and keep us together. We shall then see our object, and our ears will be legally shut against the schemes of an intriguing, as well as a cruel enemy. We shall then too be on a proper footing to treat with Britain; for there is reason to conclude, that the pride of that court will be less hurt by treating with the American states for terms of peace, than with those she denominates "rebellious subjects," for terms of accommodation. It is our delaying it that encourages her to hope for conquest, and our backwardness tends only to prolong the war. As we have, without any good effect therefrom, withheld our trade to obtain a redress of our grievances, let us now try the alternative, by independently redressing them ourselves, and then offering to open the trade. The mercantile and reasonable part in England will be still with us; because, peace with trade, is preferable to war without it. And if this offer is not accepted, other courts may be applied to. On these grounds I rest the matter. And as no offer hath yet been made to refute the doctrine contained in the former editions of this pamphlet, it is a negative proof, that either the doctrine cannot be refuted, or, that the party in favor of it are too numerous to be opposed. Wherefore instead of gazing at each other with suspicious or doubtful curiosity, let each of us hold out to his neighbor the hearty hand of friendship, and unite in drawing a line, which, like an act of oblivion, shall bury in forgetfulness every former dissension. Let the names of Whig and Tory be extinct; and let none other be heard among us, than those of a good citizen, an open and resolute friend, and a virtuous supporter of the rights of mankind and of the free and independent states of America.

Thomas Paine, *Common Sense*, January 1776.

The Virginia Declaration of Rights

Although the Declaration of Independence outlined the reasons for separation from England, it did not lay out any plan for governing the new nation. That would not come until the creation of the U.S. Constitution in 1787. Until then, the governments of the various colonies drafted their own constitutions. Using legislative philosophy that would appear in the declaration as well as employing concepts inherent to English common law, the Virginia constitution was perhaps the most significant of the colonial constitutions. The reason for this is the Virginia Declaration of Rights, an attached bill of rights written chiefly by George Mason and adopted by the Virginia Convention on June 12, 1776. The Declaration of Rights sets down governing principles and records specific rights of citizens that could never be abridged. The Virginia Declaration of Rights was so well regarded that it would serve as a model for the U.S. Bill of Rights as well as the Declaration of the Rights of Man, an influential document on individual liberties that was drafted during the French Revolution.

I. That all men are by nature equally free and independent, and have certain inherent rights, of which, when they enter into a state of society, they cannot, by any compact, deprive or divest their posterity; namely, the enjoyment of life and liberty, with the means of acquiring and possessing property, and pursuing and obtaining happiness and safety.

II. That all power is vested in, and consequently derived from, the people; that magistrates are their trustees and servants, and at all times amenable to them.

III. That government is, or ought to be, instituted for the common benefit, protection, and security of the people, nation or community; of all the various modes and forms of government that is best, which is capable of producing the greatest degree of happiness and safety and is most effectually secured against the danger of maladministration; and that, whenever any government shall be found inadequate or contrary to these purposes, a majority of the community hath an indubitable, unalienable, and indefeasible right to reform, alter or abolish it, in such manner as shall be judged most conducive to the public weal.

IV. That no man, or set of men, are entitled to exclusive or separate emoluments or privileges from the community, but in consideration of public services; which, not being descendible, neither ought the offices of magistrate, legislator, or judge be hereditary.

V. That the legislative and executive powers of the state should be separate and distinct from the judicative; and, that the members of the two first may be restrained from oppression by feeling and participating the burthens of the people, they should, at fixed periods, be reduced to a private station, return into that body from which they were originally taken, and the vacancies be supplied by fre-

quent, certain, and regular elections in which all, or any part of the former members, to be again eligible, or ineligible, as the laws shall direct.

VI. That elections of members to serve as representatives of the people in assembly ought to be free; and that all men, having sufficient evidence of permanent common interest with, and attachment to, the community have the right of suffrage and cannot be taxed or deprived of their property for public uses without their own consent or that of their representatives so elected, nor bound by any law to which they have not, in like manner, assented, for the public good.

VII. That all power of suspending laws, or the execution of laws, by any authority without consent of the representatives of the people is injurious to their rights and ought not to be exercised.

VIII. That in all capital or criminal prosecutions a man hath a right to demand the cause and nature of his accusation to be confronted with the accusers and witnesses, to call for evidence in his favor, and to a speedy trial by an impartial jury of his vicinage, without whose unanimous consent he cannot be found guilty, nor can he be compelled to give evidence against himself; that no man be deprived of his liberty except by the law of the land or the judgement of his peers.

IX. That excessive bail ought not to be required, nor excessive fines imposed; nor cruel and unusual punishments inflicted.

X. That general warrants, whereby any officer or messenger may be commanded to search suspected places without evidence of a fact committed, or to seize any person or persons not named, or whose offense is not particularly described and supported by evidence, are grievous and oppressive and ought not to be granted.

XI. That in controversies respecting property and in suits between man and man, the ancient trial by jury is preferable to any other and ought to be held sacred.

XII. That the freedom of the press is one of the greatest bulwarks of liberty and can never be restrained but by despotic governments.

XIII. That a well regulated militia, composed of the body of the people, trained to arms, is the proper, natural, and safe defense of a free state; that standing armies, in time of peace, should be avoided as dangerous to liberty; and that, in all cases, the military should be under strict subordination to, and be governed by, the civil power.

XIV. That the people have a right to uniform government; and therefore, that no government separate from, or independent of, the government of Virginia, ought to be erected or established within the limits thereof.

XV. That no free government, or the blessings of liberty, can be preserved to any people but by a firm adherence to justice, moderation, temperance, frugality, and virtue and by frequent recurrence to fundamental principles.

XVI. That religion, or the duty which we owe to our Creator and the manner of discharging it, can be directed by reason and conviction, not by force or violence; and therefore, all men are equally entitled to the free exercise of religion, according to the dictates of conscience; and that it is the mutual duty of all to practice Christian forbearance, love, and charity toward each other.

Virginia Declaration of Rights, adopted June 12, 1776.

Notes from Congressional Debate

In June 1776 the Continental Congress met for a second time in Philadelphia. The question before the delegates was not whether to reconcile with England but whether to declare an immediate separation. The decision was difficult since many members did not feel the colonies could stand on their own and support a war effort against their parent nation. One of the prime concerns was determining how America could finance its bid for independence. Thomas Jefferson, serving as a delegate from Virginia, stayed quiet during the debates but carefully took notes on the various arguments.

On July 2 the Congress voted to declare America an independent nation. Expecting this outcome, the delegates had already asked Jefferson to draft a document declaring the colonies' intent. Jefferson was chosen because he was well regarded as a lawyer and as a scholar of literature and composition. Two days after the vote was taken, the Second Continental Congress adopted his Declaration of Independence.

The Declaration of Independence (below) and its author, Thomas Jefferson (left), are enduring symbols of the United States.

IN CONGRESS. JULY 4, 1776.

The unanimous Declaration of the thirteen united States of America,

THE DECLARATION OF INDEPENDENCE.
FIG. 116: Congress passed the resolution calling for independence on July 2, 1776. On July 4, the formal Declaration was adopted. This illustration reproduces the formal Declaration engrossed on parchment, probably by Timothy Matlack of Philadelphia, and signed by most members of Congress on August 2, 1776.

Friday, June 7, 1776, the Delegates from Virginia moved in obedience to instructions from their constituents that the Congress should declare that these United colonies are & of right ought to be free & independent states . . . that measures should be immediately taken for procuring the assistance of foreign powers, and a Confederation be formed to bind the colonies more closely together.

That such a secession would weaken us more than could be compensated by any foreign alliance. . . .

That France & Spain had reason to be jealous of that rising power which would one day certainly strip them of all their American possessions:

That it was more likely they [France and Spain] should form a connection with the British court, who, if they should find themselves unable otherwise to extricate themselves from their difficulties, would agree to a partition of our territories, restoring Canada to France, & the Floridas to Spain, to accomplish for themselves a recovery of these colonies:

That it would not be long before we should receive certain information of the disposition of the French court, from the agent [Silas Deane] . . . sent to Paris for that purpose:

That if this disposition should be favorable, by waiting the event of the present campaign, which we all hope would be successful, we should have reason to expect an alliance on better terms. . . .

That a declaration of Independence alone could render it consistent with European delicacy for European powers to treat with us, or even to receive an Ambassador from us. . . .

That tho' France & Spain may be jealous of our rising power, they must think it will be much more formidable with the addition of Great Britain; and will therefore see it their interest to prevent a coalition. . . .

That the present campaign may be unsuccessful, & therefore we had better propose an alliance while our affairs wear a hopeful aspect:

That to wait the event of this campaign will certainly work delay, because during this summer France may assist us effectually by cutting off those supplies of provisions from England & Ireland on which the enemy's armies here are to depend; or by setting in motion the great power they have collected in the West Indies, & calling our enemy to the defence of the possessions they have there. . . .

And that the only misfortune is that we did not enter into alliance with France six months sooner, as besides opening their ports for the vent [sale] of our last year's produce, they might have marched an army into Germany and prevented the petty princes there from selling their unhappy subjects [the Hessian mercenaries] to subdue us.

Thomas Jefferson, notes from Continental Congress debate, June 1776.

Congress Votes for Independence

On July 3, 1776, John Adams wrote to his wife, Abigail, informing her that the Second Continental Congress voted the previous day to sever its ties with England and seek independence. After a month of debates, twelve of the thirteen colonies had finally agreed to support American independence; only New York abstained from casting its vote. Adams, a delegate from Massachusetts, had favored independence all along, and in his letter to his wife, he is optimistic that America—under the guiding hand of Providence—will soon be a free country.

Yesterday the greatest Question was decided, which ever was debated in America, and a greater perhaps, never was or will be decided among Men. A Resolution was passed without one dissenting Colony "that these united Colonies, are, and of right ought to be free and independent States, and as such, they have, and of Right ought to have full Power to make

John Adams, a Massachusetts delegate, supported the idea of gaining independence from England.

War, conclude Peace, establish Commerce, and to do all the other Acts and Things, which other States may rightfully do." You will see in a few days a Declaration setting forth the Causes, which have impell'd Us to this mighty Revolution, and the Reasons which will justify it, in the Sight of God and Man. A Plan of Confederation will be taken up in a few days.

When I look back to the Year 1761, and recollect the Argument concerning Writs of Assistance, in the Superiour Court, which I have hitherto considered as the Commencement of the Controversy, between Great Britain and America, and run through the whole Period from that Time to this, and recollect the series of political Events, the Chain of Causes and Effects, I am surprised at the Suddenness,

as well as Greatness of this Revolution. Britain has been fill'd with Folly, and America with Wisdom, at least this is my Judgment.—Time must determine. It is the Will of Heaven, that the two Countries should be sundered forever. It may be the Will of Heaven that America shall suffer Calamities still more wasting and Distresses yet more dreadfull. If this is to be the Case, it will have this good Effect, at least: it will inspire Us with many Virtues, which We have not, and correct many Errors, Follies, and Vices, which threaten to disturb, dishonour, and destroy Us.—The Furnace of Affliction produces Refinement, in States as well as Individuals. And the new Governments we are assuming, in every Part, will require a Purification from our Vices, and an Augmentation of our Virtues or they will be no Blessings. The People will have unbounded Power. And the People are extreamly addicted to Corruption and Venality, as well as the Great.—I am not without Apprehensions from this Quarter. But I must submit all my Hopes and Fears, to an overruling Providence, in which, unfashionable as the Faith may be, I firmly believe.

John Adams, letter to Abigail Adams, July 3, 1776.

The Declaration of Independence

When Thomas Jefferson was given the task of drafting the new nation's Declaration of Inde-

pendence, he seemed to have no knowledge of how significant the document would become. He worked quickly and went through a few drafts. When he submitted the work for the approval of the Second Continental Congress, the various delegates made several alterations and cuts. Benjamin Franklin tried to bolster Jefferson's spirits as his words were deleted or changed, but Jefferson sat silently throughout the ordeal. He never publicly challenged the changes made to his original document, but privately he believed his words had been "mutilated" by the Congress.

Benjamin Franklin and other delegates revise Thomas Jefferson's Declaration of Independence.

On July 4, 1776, Congress voted whether to accept the altered document. The debate lasted long into the evening. Finally, all colonies except New York endorsed the Declaration of Independence. Five days later the New York delegation ratified the document after getting approval from their colonial government. Copies of the declaration were sent out to newspapers, colonial officials, and military commanders on July 5. Soon all of colonial America received word that the union between England and its colonies was dissolved.

When in the Course of human events, it becomes necessary for one people to dissolve the political bands which have connected them with another, and to assume among the Powers of the earth, the separate and equal station to which the Laws of Nature and of Nature's God entitle them, a decent respect to the opinions of mankind requires that they should declare the causes which impel them to the separation. We hold these truths to be self-evident, that all men are created equal, that they are endowed by their Creator with certain unalienable Rights, that among these are Life, Liberty and the pursuit of Happiness. That to secure these rights, Governments are instituted among Men, deriving their just powers from the consent of the governed, That whenever any Form of Government becomes destructive of these ends, it is the Right of the People to alter or to abolish it, and to institute new Government, laying its foundation on such principles and organizing its powers in such form, as to them shall seem most likely to effect their Safety and Happiness. Prudence, indeed, will dictate that Governments long established should not be changed for light and transient causes; and accordingly all experience hath shown, that mankind are more disposed to suffer, while evils are sufferable, than to right themselves by abolishing the forms to which they are accustomed. But when a long train of abuses and usurpations, pursuing invariably the same Object evinces a design to reduce them under absolute Despotism, it is their right, it is their duty, to throw off such Government, and to provide new Guards for their future security.—Such has been the patient sufferance of these Colonies; and such is now the necessity which constrains them to alter their former Systems of Government. The history of the present King of Great Britain is a history of repeated injuries and usurpations, all having in direct object the establishment of an absolute Tyranny over these States. To prove this, let Facts be submitted to a candid world.

He has refused his Assent to Laws, the most wholesome and necessary for the public good.

He has forbidden his Governors to pass Laws of immediate and pressing importance, unless suspended in their oper-

ation till his Assent should be obtained; and when so suspended, he has utterly neglected to attend to them.

He has refused to pass other Laws for the accommodation of large districts of people, unless those people would relinquish the right of Representation in the Legislature, a right inestimable to them and formidable to tyrants only.

He has called together legislative bodies at places unusual, uncomfortable, and distant from the depository or their public Records, for the sole purpose of fatiguing them into compliance with his measures.

He has dissolved Representative Houses repeatedly, for opposing with manly firmness his invasions on the rights of the people.

He has refused for a long time, after such dissolutions, to cause others to be elected; whereby the Legislative powers, incapable of Annihilation, have returned to the People at large for their exercise; the State remaining in the mean time exposed to all the dangers of invasion from without, and convulsions within.

He has endeavoured to prevent the population of these States; for that purpose obstructing the Laws for Naturalization of Foreigners; refusing to pass others to encourage their migration hither, and raising the conditions of new Appropriations of Lands.

He has obstructed the Administration of Justice, by refusing his Assent to Laws for establishing Judiciary powers.

He has made Judges dependent on his Will alone, for the tenure of their offices, and the amount and payment of their salaries.

He has erected a multitude of New Offices, and sent hither swarms of Officers to harrass our people, and eat out their substance.

He has kept among us, in times of peace, Standing Armies, without the Consent of our legislatures.

He has affected to render the Military independent of and superior to the Civil power.

He has combined with others to subject us to a jurisdiction foreign to our constitution, and unacknowledged by our laws; giving his Assent to their Acts of pretended Legislation:

For quartering large bodies of armed troops among us:

For protecting them, by a mock Trial, from Punishment for any Murders which they should commit on the Inhabitants of these States:

For cutting off our Trade with all parts of the world:

For imposing Taxes on us without our Consent:

For depriving us in many cases, of the benefits of Trial by Jury:

For transporting us beyond Seas to be tried for pretended offenses:

For abolishing the free System of English Laws in a neighboring Province, establishing therein an Arbitrary government, and enlarging its Boundaries so as to render it at once an example and fit instrument for introducing the same absolute rule into these Colonies:

For taking away our Charters, abolishing our most valuable Laws, and altering fundamentally the Forms of our Governments:

For suspending our own Legislatures, and declaring themselves invested with power to legislate for us in all cases whatsoever.

He has abdicated Government here, by declaring us out of his Protection and waging War against us.

He has plundered our seas, ravaged our Coasts, burnt our towns, and destroyed the lives of our people.

He is at this time transporting large Armies of foreign Mercenaries to compleat the works of death, desolation and tyranny, already begun with circumstances of Cruelty & perfidy scarcely paralleled in the most barbarous ages, and totally unworthy the Head of a civilized nation.

He has constrained our fellow Citizens taken Captive on the high Seas to bear Arms against their Country, to become the executioners of their friends and Brethren, or to fall themselves by their Hands.

He has excited domestic insurrections amongst us, and has endeavoured to bring on the inhabitants of our frontiers, the merciless Indian Savages, whose known rule of warfare, is an undistinguished destruction of all ages, sexes and conditions.

In every state of these Oppressions We have Petitioned for Redress in the most humble terms: Our repeated Petitions have been answered only by repeated injury. A Prince, whose character is thus marked by every act which may define a Tyrant, is unfit to be the ruler of a free people.

Nor have We been wanting in attentions to our Brittish brethren. We have warned them from time to time of attempts by their legislature to extend an unwarrantable jurisdiction over us. We have reminded them of the circumstances of our emigration and settlement here. We have appealed to their native justice and magnanimity, and we have conjured them by the ties of our common kindred to disavow these usurpations, which, would inevitably interrupt our connections and correspondence. They too have been deaf to the voice of justice and of consanguinity. We must, therefore, acquiesce in the necessity, which denounces our Separation, and hold them, as we hold the rest of mankind, Enemies in War, in Peace Friends.

We, Therefore, the Representatives of the United States of America, in General Congress, Assembled, appealing to the Supreme Judge of the world for the rectitude of our intentions, do, in the Name, and by Authority of the good People of these Colonies, solemnly publish and declare, That these United Colonies are, and of Right ought to be Free and Independent States; that they are Absolved from all Allegiance to the British Crown, and that all political connection between them and the State of Great Britain, is and ought to be totally disolved; and that as Free and Independent States, they have full Power to levy War, conclude Peace, contract Alliances, establish Commerce, and to do all other Acts and Things which Independent States may of right do. And for the support of this Declaration, with a firm reliance on the protection of Divine Providence, we mutually pledge to each other our Lives, our Fortunes and our sacred Honor.

Thomas Jefferson, Declaration of Independence, July 4, 1776.

New York Reacts to Independence

Copies of the Declaration of Independence reached the various towns and cities of colonial America at different times. As the journal of Lieutenant Isaac Bangs attests, the declaration arrived in New York on July 9, 1776. Bangs, a colonial officer, witnessed the jubilation of his brigade when the document was read. That evening, he saw the effect the news had on the citizens of New York. Bangs watched as a crowd pulled down an equestrian statue of King George III that resided in a city square. The lieutenant reports that the lead in the statue was then melted down to make ammunition for colonial soldiers. The statue is reputed to have yielded forty-two thousand bullets, all of which Bangs expected would make "deep impressions" on British soldiers and Tory sympathizers when fired from colonial muskets.

July 8, 1776. Nothing material happened.

9th. In the afternoon went to the City & engaged a Gentleman to teach a Number

The colonists dismantle a statue of King George III in celebration of their newfound freedom.

of us the French Language. Visited Miss Betsy Grim & Lieut. Hayward.

This afternoon the Declaration of the Independence of the 13 American States was read to the Several Brigades. It was received with Joy, which they severally testified by three Cheers.

10th. Orders were Issued for our Brigade to be in readiness at 4 o'clock tomorrow Morning for a March. We all imagined that we were designed to make an Attack upon the Enemy on Staten Island, but on farther consideration we had reason to doubt of it, as no particular Orders were Issued with Respect to our Bagage, which would be Necessary to take with us if this was the Intention of the General.

Last Night the Statue on the Bowling Green representing George Ghwelph alias George Rex . . . was pulled down by the Populace. In it were 4,000 Pounds of Lead, & a Man undertook to take of 10 oz of Gold from the Superficies, as both Man & Horse were covered with Gold Leaf. The Lead, we hear, is to be run up into Musquet Balls for the use of the Yankees, when it is hoped that the Emanations of the Leaden George will make as deep impressions in the Bodies of some of his red Coated & Torie Subjects, & that they will do the same execution in poisoning & destroying them, as the superabundant Emanations of the Folly & pretended Goodness of the real George have made upon their Minds, which have effectually poisoned & destroyed their Souls, that they are not worthy to be ranked with any Beings who have any Pretensions to the Principles of Virtue & Justice; but would to God that the unhappy contest might be ended without putting us to the disagreeable Necessity of sending them to dwell with those beings for the Company of whom alone their Tempers & dispositions are now suitable.

Isaac Bangs, excerpt from his journal.

Strictures upon the Declaration

Thomas Hutchinson had served as the acting governor of Massachusetts until 1774. He was loyal to the Crown and believed that the rebellion that was growing in the colonies even then was the work of a few agitators who were deceiving the majority of content colonists with trumped up examples of parliamentary abuses. Hutchinson claimed that those who fomented rebellion had always had it in their minds to declare colonial independence; their complaints that England was not listening to legitimate colonial grievances were merely a smokescreen to hide their real intent.

Hutchinson had retired to England by the time word of the Declaration of Independence made its way across the Atlantic. Having heard the arguments before, he was not surprised at the statements of colonial discontent. Therefore, unlike much of England, Hutchinson did not react to the declaration with indignation. Instead, he wrote out what he called his Strictures upon the Declaration of the Congress at Philadelphia, *a rational redress of the arguments contained in the document. In this excerpt from his* Strictures *(which originally was written as a letter to an English lord) Hutchinson relates the colonial grievances as listed in the declaration, followed by his own analysis of their faulty logic.*

They begin, my Lord, with a false hypothesis, That the Colonies are one distinct people, and the kingdom another, connected by political bands. The Colonies, politically considered, never were a distinct people from the kingdom. There never has been but one political band, and that was just the same before the first Colonists emigrated as it has been ever since, the Supreme Legislative Authority, which hath essential right, and is indispensably bound to keep all parts of the Empire entire, until there may be a separation consistent with the general good of the Empire, of which good, from the nature of government, this authority must be the sole judge. I should therefore be impertinent, if I attempted to shew [show] in what case a whole people may be justified in rising up in oppugnation [fight or battle] to the powers of government, altering or abolishing them, and substituting, in whole or in part, new powers in their stead; or in what sense all men are created equal; or how far life, liberty, and the pursuit of happiness may be said to be unalienable; only I could wish to ask the Delegates of Maryland, Virginia, and the Carolinas, how their Constituents justify the depriving more than an hundred thousand Africans of their rights to liberty, and the pursuit of happiness, and in some degree to their lives, if these rights are so absolutely unalienable; nor shall I attempt to confute the absurd notions of government, or to expose the equivocal or inconclusive expressions contained in this

Declaration; but rather to shew the false representation made of the facts which are alleged to be the evidence of injuries and usurpations, and the special motives to Rebellion. There are many of them, with design, left obscure; for as soon as they are developed, instead of justifying, they rather aggravate the criminality of this Revolt.

The first in order, He [King George III] has refused his assent to laws the most wholesome and necessary for the public good; is of so general a nature that it is not possible to conjecture to what laws or to what Colonies it refers. I remember no laws which any Colony has been restrained from passing, so as to cause any complaint of grievance, except those for issuing a fraudulent paper-currency, and making it a legal tender; but this is a restraint which for many years past has been laid on Assemblies by an act of Parliament, since which such laws cannot have been offered to the King for his allowance. I therefore believe this to be a general charge, without any particulars to support it; fit enough to be placed at the head of a list of imaginary grievances.

The laws of England are or ought to be the laws of its Colonies. To prevent a deviation further than the local circumstances of any Colony may make necessary, all Colony laws are to be laid before the King; and if disallowed, they then become of no force. . . .

He [the king] has dissolved Representatives Houses repeatedly for opposing with manly firmness his Invasions on the Rights of the People.

Contentions between Governors and their Assemblies have caused dissolutions of such Assemblies, I suppose, in all the Colonies, in former as well as later times. I recollect but one instance of the dissolution of an Assembly by special order from the King, and that was in Massachuset's Bay. In 1768, the House of Representatives passed a vote or resolve, in prosecution of the plan of Independence, incompatible with the subordination of the Colonies to the supreme authority of the Empire; and directed their Speaker to send a copy of it in circular letters to the Assemblies of the other Colonies, inviting them to avow the principles of the resolve, and to join in supporting them. No Government can long subsist, which admits of combinations of the subordinate powers against the supreme. This proceeding was therefore, justly deemed highly unwarrantable; and indeed it was the beginning of that unlawful confederacy, which has gone on until it has caused at least a temporary Revolt of all the Colonies which joined in it.

The Governor was instructed to require the House of Representatives, in their next Session to rescind or disavow this resolve, and if they refused, to dissolve them, as the only way to prevent their prosecuting the plan of Rebellion. They delayed a definitive answer, and he indulged them, until they had finished all the business of the Province, and then appeared this manly firmness in a rude answer and a peremptory refusal to comply with the King's demand. Thus, my Lord, the regular use of the prerogative in suppressing a begun Revolt, is urged as a grievance to justify the Revolt . . .

He has erected a Multitude of new offices and sent hither Swarms of officers, to harass our people and eat out their subsistence.

I know of no new offices erected in America in the present reign, excepted those of the Commissioners of the Customs and their dependents. Five Commissioners were appointed, and four Surveyors General dismissed; perhaps fifteen or twenty clerks and under officers were necessary for this board more than the Surveyors had occasion for before. . . . Thirty or forty additional officers in the whole Continent, are the Swarms which eat out the subsistence of the boasted number of three millions of people. . . .

He has kept among us, in times of peace, standing armies, without the consent of our legislatures.

This is too nugatory [inconsequential] to deserve any remark. He has kept no armies among them without the consent of the Supreme Legislature. It is begging the question, to suppose that this authority was not sufficient without the aid of their own Legislatures. . . .

For quartering large bodies of armed troops among us.

When troops were employed in America, in the last reign, to protect the Colonies against French invasion, it was necessary to provide against mutiny and desertion, and to secure proper quarters. Temporary Acts of Parliament were passed for that purpose, and submitted to in the Colonies. Upon the peace, raised ideas took place in the Colonies, of their own importance, and caused a reluctance against Parliamentary authority, and an opposition to the Acts for quartering troops, not because the provision made was in itself unjust or unequal, but because they were Acts of a Parliament whose authority was denied. The provision was as similar to that in England as the state of the Colonies would admit. . . .

For imposing taxes on us without our consent.

How often has your Lordship heard it said, that the Americans are willing to submit to the authority of Parliament in all cases except that of taxes? Here we have a declaration made to the world of the causes which have impelled to a separation. We are to presume that it contains all which they that publish it are able to say in support of a separation, and that if any one cause was distinguished from another, special notice would be taken of it. That of taxes seems to have been in danger of being forgot. It comes in late, and in as slight a manner as is possible. And, I know, my Lord, that these men, in the early days of their opposition to Parliament, have acknowledged that they pitched upon this subject of taxes, because it was most alarming to the people, every man perceiving immediately that he is personally affected by it; and it has, therefore, in all communities, always been a subject more dangerous to government than any other, to make innovation in; but as their friends in England had fell in with the idea that Parliament could have no right to tax them because not represented, they thought it best it should be believed they were willing to submit to other acts of legislation until this point of taxes could be gained; owning at the same time, that they could find no fundamentals in the English Constitution, which made representation more necessary in acts for taxes, than acts for any other purpose; and that the world must have a mean opinion of their understanding, if they should rebel rather than pay a duty of three-pence per pound on tea, and yet be content to submit to an act which restrained them from making a nail to shoe their own horses. . . .

They have, my Lord, in their late address to the people of Great Britain, fully avowed these principles of Independence, by declaring they will pay no obedience to the laws of the Supreme Legislature; they have also pretended, that these laws were the mandates or edicts of the Ministers, not the acts of a constitutional legislative power, and have endeavoured to persuade such as they called their British Brethren, to justify the Rebellion begun in America; and from thence they expected a general convulsion in the Kingdom, and that measures

to compel a submission would in this way be obstructed. These expectations failing, after they had gone too far in acts of Rebellion to hope for impunity, they were under the necessity of a separation, and of involving themselves, and all over whom they had usurped authority, in the distresses and horrors of war against that power from which they revolted, and against all who continued in their subjection and fidelity to it. . . .

Suffer me, my Lord, before I close this Letter, to observe, that though the professed reason for publishing the Declaration was a decent respect to the opinions of mankind, yet the real design was to reconcile the people of America to that Independence, which always before, they had been made to believe was not intended. This design has too well succeeded. The people have not observed the fallacy in reasoning from the whole to part; nor the absurdity of making the governed to be governors. From a disposition to receive willingly complaints against Rulers, facts misrepresented have passed without examining. Discerning men have concealed their sentiments, because under the present free government in America, no man may, by writing or speaking, contradict any part of this Declaration, without being deemed an enemy to his country, and exposed to the rage and fury of the populace.

Thomas Hutchinson, *Strictures upon the Declaration of the Congress at Philadelphia*, 1776. Courtesy of the Old South Association, Old South Meeting-house, Boston, Massachusetts.

We Have No Other Alternative than Independence

Samuel Adams was a Boston politician and a fierce advocate of American independence. His vocal opposition to Parliament's "interference" in the colonies was well known to the British, who considered Adams a dangerous nuisance. Adams also served as a delegate to the Con-tinental Congress, in which he continually argued for rebellion over appeasement with Britain.

When the Second Continental Congress ratified the Declaration of Independence, Adams took to the streets to explain the significance of the document to the public. In the following extract from a speech delivered at the State House in Philadelphia, Pennsylvania, on August 1, 1776, Adams preaches the gospel of independence. The large crowd that was said to have attended the speech was most likely captivated by Adams's famous fiery oratory style.

Samuel Adams argued against appeasement of Britain's demands.

The doctrine of dependence on Great Britain is, I believe, generally exploded; but as I would attend to the honest weakness of the simplest of men, you will pardon me if I offer a few words on that subject.

We are now on this continent, to the astonishment of the world, three millions of souls united in one cause. We have large armies, well disciplined and appointed, with commanders inferior to none in military skill, and superior in activity and zeal. We are furnished with arsenals and stores beyond our most sanguine expectations, and foreign nations are waiting to crown our success by their alliances. There are instances of, I would say, an almost astonishing providence in our favor; our success has staggered our enemies, and almost given faith to infidels; so we may truly say it is not our own arm which has saved us.

The hand of Heaven appears to have led us on to be, perhaps, humble instruments and means in the great providential dispensation which is completing. We have fled from the political Sodom; let us not look back lest we perish and become a monument of infamy and derision to the world [an analogy drawn from a wicked city of the Bible and the wife of Lot who, fleeing the city, looked back and was turned into a pillar of salt]. For can we ever expect more unanimity and a better preparation for defense; more infatuation of counsel among our enemies, and more valor and zeal among ourselves? The same force and resistance which are sufficient to procure us our liberties will secure us a glorious independence and support us in the dignity of free imperial States. . . .

If there is any man so base or so weak as to prefer a dependence on Great Britain to the dignity and happiness of living a member of a free and independent nation, let me tell him that necessity now demands what the generous principle of patriotism should have dictated.

We have no other alternative than independence, or the most ignominious and galling servitude. The legions of our enemies thicken on our plains; desolation and death mark their bloody career, while the mangled corpses of our countrymen seem to cry out to us as a voice from heaven. . . .

You have now in the field armies sufficient to repel the whole force of your enemies and their base and mercenary auxiliaries. The hearts of your soldiers beat high with the spirit of freedom; they are animated with the justice of their cause, and while they grasp their swords can look up to Heaven for assistance. Your adversaries are composed of wretches who laugh at the rights of humanity, who turn religion into derision, and would, for higher wages, direct their swords against their leaders or their country. Go on, then, in your generous enterprise with gratitude to Heaven for past success, and confidence of it in the future. For my own part I ask no greater blessing than to share with you the common danger and common glory.

Samuel Adams, speech given before the Pennsylvania State House, August 1, 1776.

Chapter 4

Campaigns 1776–1778

In the early years of the Revolutionary War, the British general William Howe devised a strategy that he hoped would break the rebel resistance in the colonies. Knowing the value of rivers and other waterways for rapidly moving troops in North America (a lesson learned during the French and Indian Wars), Howe determined to launch an invasion of New York in order to seize the Hudson Valley and its significant series of rivers and lakes that stretched along an axis roughly from New York City to Quebec, Canada. In holding this vital corridor, Howe hoped he would separate the troublesome New England colonies from the southern colonies, where opposition forces were not as strong.

George Washington expected an attack in New York but was not sure where Howe would strike. Washington was also acutely aware that he did not have the manpower to overcome Howe's invasion force. Although on paper he had twenty-eight thousand men enlisted, at any time Washington could only count on nineteen thousand to muster for service, and most of these were poorly trained militia who would often flee in the face of disciplined British regulars or their German mercenaries. Washington's strategy was to play a waiting game. He would hold strong defensive positions, delaying Howe's troops when possible, and would attack only when surprise and the majority of numbers were on his side. This strategy, however, was double-edged. Delaying the British usually meant fighting and retreating to save troop strength. This most likely gave the battlefield victories to Howe and reduced colonial morale. But it also meant frustrating the British commanders, who could never achieve a total victory in which the enemy forces were utterly destroyed.

Indeed, this was the pattern of the battles in and around New York. Howe landed his thirty-two thousand men near New York City on July 3, 1776. He swiftly routed colonial forces at Long Island and forced Washington to give up the city entirely in September. Washington fell back in the face of Howe's expected advance. Howe continued his advance, seizing colonial forts along the Hudson and even sending General Henry Clinton on a naval maneuver that captured Rhode Island unopposed. Washington decided to abandon lower New York and gathered his remaining strength in Hackensack, New Jersey. By the close of the year, Washington's army had dwindled. Half of his troops, mostly militia outfits, deserted and returned home. His subordinate generals were skeptical of his leadership, blaming him for the recent series of defeats. Even

General William Howe of Great Britain believed he could gain control over the colonists.

members of the Continental Congress had second thoughts, especially given the fact that with Howe in control of New York, the road to Philadelphia was open. With everything against him and his reputation on the line, Washington decided to gamble on his leadership and his remaining men.

In December 1776 Washington gathered seven thousand men in Pennsylvania and ferried them across the Delaware River intending to attack the towns of Trenton and Bordentown in New Jersey. General Howe had left a detachment of three thousand Hessian mercenaries to guard these posts while he pulled the main British force back to New York to wait out the winter. Washington scheduled his attack to fall on Christmas night in hopes that the Hessians would be celebrating and unready for battle. His expectations were fulfilled, and the Hessians surrendered after token resistance. As quickly as he had come, Washington again crossed the Delaware before the British could muster their army for a reprisal.

The victories in New Jersey were important for the colonial cause. They illustrated that Washington's ragtag army could defeat a better-trained enemy, and they proved that Washington was a capable tactician who, despite handicaps, could achieve military success. These qualities attracted not only the attention of colonists but also the inquisitive eyes of foreign powers such as France and Spain. Both of these nations considered Britain a rival—especially France, which had fought many

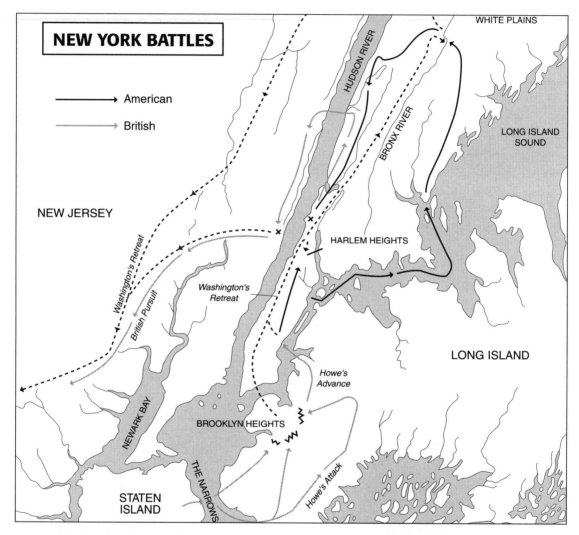

NEW YORK BATTLES

→ American

→ British

WHITE PLAINS

HUDSON RIVER

BRONX RIVER

LONG ISLAND SOUND

NEW JERSEY

Washington's Retreat

British Pursuit

Washington's Retreat

HARLEM HEIGHTS

LONG ISLAND

Howe's Advance

NEWARK BAY

BROOKLYN HEIGHTS

THE NARROWS

Howe's Attack

STATEN ISLAND

wars with England over the last two centuries—and neither was sorry to see English authority in the New World jeopardized. The Continental Congress had sent delegations to France early in the war to secure loans and military assistance. Although France granted this assistance, King Louis XVI was hesitant to bring his nation back into conflict with England. He was unsure if the Americans could stage a rebellion for any length of time, and he did not want French soldiers carrying the brunt of the military duties so far from home. He did, however, allow French military officers to volunteer to help train and fight with the colonials. Many of these men—such as the Marquis de Lafayette—did provide invaluable service to the Americans, especially in shaping the Continental army into a fighting force that could face the disciplined British on equal terms.

With supplies and cash loans granted from France and Spain, the colonial army fought on through 1777. As Washington and Howe sparred in Pennsylvania, British general John Burgoyne was ordered to march on Albany, New York, from his base in Canada. With Howe's army holding the southern part of the Hudson and Burgoyne marching down the northern extreme, the two would meet and cut off New England as planned. Burgoyne set off optimistically in June, but his army soon bogged down in the thick woods along the route. Many of his loyalist recruits de-

serted him, as did several of the Indian allies. He also had severed communications with Canada, leaving his dwindling army isolated in the American wilderness. On September 19, 1777, Burgoyne met a colonial force commanded by General Horatio Gates near Saratoga, New York. With an army of fewer than six thousand men, he attacked Gates's well-entrenched positions in a series of battles that lasted into October. Throughout the engagements Burgoyne could not gain an advantage and his food supplies were nearly exhausted. Meanwhile, the American forces grew in strength, eventually encircling the British with nearly twenty thousand men. In a losing situation, Burgoyne surrendered.

News of the victory at Saratoga bolstered patriot morale in the colonies. Perhaps more significantly, it proved to France's King Louis that Americans were determined to win their freedom. He began negotiations with the colonies to bring France and its military into the war against England. On the eve of 1778, the colonial seat of government, Philadelphia, was in the hands of the British, but the tide in the American Revolution had shifted in favor of the rebels fighting for independence.

Colonial forces under the command of General Horatio Gates (pictured) defeated the British at Saratoga.

The Mohawk Remain Loyal to England

When war broke out in colonial America, the Native Americans who lived in or around

Captain Joseph Brant, a Mohawk Indian, initially sided with the British.

Joseph Brant was a Mohawk Indian who served as England's ambassador to the Iroquois Nation. Brant had been invited to England in March 1776 and had been made a captain in the British army. He met the secretary for the colonies, Lord George Germain, and made the following speech that pledged Mohawk loyalty for England's commitment to stop further settlement of Iroquois land. Germain agreed to the terms but ultimately was powerless to enforce them. English troops were needed to fight the war, not settle boundary disputes.

Brant returned to America and raised roughly one thousand Iroquois warriors to assist General John Burgoyne's soldiers in New York. Burgoyne's campaign was a disaster, and many Native Americans died in its poorly planned and poorly executed battles. The Iroquois were disgusted at the failures and eventually abandoned Burgoyne and the British cause.

conflicted regions were pulled into the fighting. Indeed, both the British and the colonials made overtures to Indian tribes to garner their sympathies. The colonials, for the most part, tried to keep the Native Americans neutral. The young American government did not have enough money to recruit Indians to its cause, and the colonials generally felt that they had enough men to do the fighting without Indian aid.

England, however, had more money than men. It offered payments and trade goods to entice native tribes to join the war against the colonists. Although many tribal chiefs preferred to stay out of a contest among Europeans, those who did aid the British typically did so not only for cash but also for the promise that England would restrain colonial settlers from encroaching on Indian land.

Brother Gorah.

We have crossed the great Lake and come to this kingdom with our Superintendant Col. Johnson from our Confederacy the Six Nations and their Allies, that we might see our Father the Great King, and join in informing him, his Councillors and wise men, of the good intentions of the Indians our brethren, and of their attachment to His Majesty and his Government.

Brother. The Disturbances in America give great trouble to all our Nations, as many strange stories have been told to us by the people in that country. The Six Nations who always loved the King, sent a number of their Chiefs and Warriors with their Superintendant to Canada last summer, where they engaged their allies to join with them in the defence of that country, and when it was invaded by the New England people, they alone defeated them.

Brother. In that engagement we had several of our best Warriors killed and wounded, and the Indians think it very hard they should have been so deceived by the White people in that country, the enemy returning in great numbers, and no White people supporting the Indians, they were obliged to retire to their villages and sit still. We now Brother hope to see these bad children chastised, and that we may be enabled to tell the Indians, who have always been faithfull and ready to assist the King, what His Majesty intends.

Brother. The Mohocks our particular Nation, have on all occasions shewn their zeal and loyalty to the Great King; yet they have been very badly treated by his people in that country, the City of Albany laying an unjust claim to the lands on which our Lower Castle is built, as one Klock and others do to those of Conijoharrie our Upper Village. We have been often assured by our late great friend Sir William Johnson [the English Superintendent of Indian Affairs until 1774] who never deceived us, and we know he was told so that the King and wise men here would do us justice; but this notwithstanding all our applications has never been done, and it makes us very uneasy. We also feel for the distress in which our Brethren on the Susquehanna are

likely to be involved by a mistake made in the Boundary we settled in 1768. This also our Superintendant has laid before the King, and we beg it may be remembered. And also concerning Religion and the want of Ministers of the Church of England, he knows the designs of those bad people and informs us he has laid the same before the King. We have only therefore to request that his Majesty will attend to this matter: it troubles our Nation & they cannot sleep easy in their beds. Indeed it is very hard when we have let the Kings subjects have so much of our lands for so little value, they should want to cheat us in this manner of the small spots we have left for our women and children to live on. We are tired out in making complaints & getting no redress. We therefore hope that the Assurances now given us by the Superintendant may take place, and that he may have it in his power to procure us justice.

Brother. We shall truly report all that we hear from you, to the Six Nations at our return. We are well informed there has been many Indians in this Country who came without any authority, from their own, and gave much trouble. We desire Brother to tell you this is not our case. We are warriors known to all the Nations, and are now here by approbation of many of them, whose sentiments we speak.

Brother. We hope these things will be considered and that the King or his great men will give us such an answer as will make our hearts light and glad before we go, and strengthen our hands, so that we may join our Superintendant Col. Johnson in giving satisfaction to all our Nations, when we report to them, on our return; for which purpose we hope soon to be accommodated with a passage.

Joseph Brant, speech to Lord Germain, March 1776.

The Colonial Defeat at Long Island

In executing his Hudson Valley campaign, England's General William Howe first directed his army to seize the city of New York and its envi-

To better defend Long Island and to protect his army, General Israel Putnam had strong fortifications built.

rons. Facing this threat, George Washington had decided to fortify the town and neighboring Long Island. Washington knew the colonial position in New York was tenuous. The British fleet commanded the waters around New York and could impose itself between the mainland and Long Island to cut the colonial forces in two. Still, the general believed the thickly wooded high ground on Long Island was strategically important.

Washington placed General Israel Putnam in charge of the island's defense. Putnam had perhaps ten thousand men to stand off the British invasion. Most were untrained militia who many colonial officers feared would run in the face of battle unless well protected. So throughout August 1776, the colonial forces built strong fortifications that fronted the entrance to New York harbor.

On August 26 General Howe began his assault on New York and Long Island. Having suffered great losses in the frontal attack during the Battle of Bunker Hill, Howe was not willing to risk another disaster. Instead of approaching the colonial defenses head on, he sent his army—primarily composed of Hessian mercenaries—to flank the enemy positions. The assault was successful, and the untrained colonials broke and ran after losing about one thousand men. The following letter from a British field officer to his wife attests to Howe's stunning victory. Yet despite his initial success in driving the rebels from their fortifications, Howe failed to pursue and destroy the routed enemy. Washington capitalized on Howe's hesitancy and made his way to New York on the night of August 29. Taking immediate command, he directed an orderly retreat across the

East River to the mainland, saving the remnants of the colonial army.

British soldiers take control of Long Island as untrained colonials retreat.

We have had a glorious day against the rebels. We landed on this island the 22d, and that day marched toward Brookland Ferry, opposite New York, where this island is separated from the town by the East River, which is about three quarters of a mile over.

We took post within musket shot of their un-finished works. The troops were all on fire to force their lines, but Gen. Howe, in whose conduct the utmost prudence and vigilance have been united, would not permit it.

It was not till eight o'clock at night on the 26th that we received our orders to at-tack, and at eleven the whole army was in motion. The reserve, commanded by Lord Cornwallis, the first brigade of which our regiment makes a part, and the light infantry of the army, the whole under the command of General Clinton, marched by the right. The road to the right, after a march of about seven miles, brought us to an easy and undefended ascent of the hills, which we possessed at daybreak, and continued our rout, gained the rear of the rebels: and while the Hessians and the rest of the army amused them in front and on the left, the grenadiers and light infantry attacked them in the rear: by this masterly maneuver the rebels were immediately thrown into general confusion, and behaved most shamefully. The numbers killed, wounded, and taken you will see in the Gazette. Some of the Hessians told me they had buried between 400 and 500 in one pit.

Such has been their panic that, on the 30th at night, they evacuated their redoubts and entrenchments, which they had retired to, on Brookland Heights, leaving us in possession of this island, which entirely commands New York. Had the works at Brookland been properly defended our motions must have been retarded at least three weeks. For my part I think matters will soon be brought to an issue.

P.S. I have just heard there has been a most dreadful fray in the town of New York. The New Englanders insisted upon setting the town on fire, and retreating. This was opposed by the New Yorkers, who were joined by the Pennsylvanians, and a battle has been the consequence in which many have lost their lives.

By the steps the General is taking, I imagine he will effectually cut off their retreat at King's Bridge, by which the island of New York is joined to the continent.

Anonymous British field officer, letter to his wife describing the Battle of Long Island, September 1, 1776.

Victory at Trenton

During the winter months of 1776, General William Howe kept his British units encamped in New York. His three thousand Hessian mercenaries were spread out over three towns in neighboring New Jersey. George Washington was eager to avenge his loss of New York, but time was running out to plan a masterstroke before the end of the year. He needed to act decisively not only to repair America's fighting reputation but also to avoid having half of his army disappear when, on December 31, the militia's terms of military enlistment were up and his fair-weather soldiers would go home.

Washington devised a bold plan to strike the enemy when it least expected. He organized seven thousand men in Pennsylvania and intended to have them ferried across the Delaware River to make a surprise raid on the Hessians at Trenton and Bordentown, New Jersey. He scheduled the attack for Christmas night, assuming that the Hessians would be celebrating and unprepared for military action.

The evening of December 25 was cold and snowy, and it took many hours for Washington's troops to cross the ice-filled Delaware. But their surprise of the Hessians was complete. Two colonial forces converged on Trenton while another advanced on Bordentown during the early hours of December 26. The Hessians sprang from their barracks and guard posts only to be shot down or captured by the Americans. In all, the Hessians suffered 50 casualties but lost another 920 men as prisoners. General Washington sent off a quick dispatch to John Hancock, president of the Continental Congress, informing him of the great victory.

I have the pleasure of congratulating you upon the success of an enterprise, which

I had formed against a detachment of the enemy lying at Trenton, and which was executed yesterday morning. The evening of the twenty-fifth I ordered the troops intended for this service to parade back to McKonkey's Ferry, that they might begin to pass as soon as it grew dark, imagining we should be able to throw them all over, with the necessary artillery, by twelve o'clock, and that we might easily arrive at Trenton by five in the morning, the distance being about nine miles. But the quantity of ice, made that night, impeded the passage of the boats so much, that it was three o'clock before the artillery could all be got over; and near four before the troops took up their line of march. This made me despair of surprising the town, as I well knew we could not reach it before the day was fairly broke. But as I was certain there was no making a retreat without being discovered and harassed on repassing the river, I determined to push on at all events. I formed my detachment into two divisions, one to march by the lower or river road, the other by the upper or Pennington road. As the divisions had nearly the same distance to march, I ordered each of them, immediately upon forcing the out-guards, to push directly into the town, that they might charge the enemy before they had time to form.

The upper division arrived at the enemy's advanced posts exactly at eight o'clock; and in three minutes after, I found, from the fire on the lower road, that the divisions had also got up. The out-guards made but small opposition, though, for their numbers, they behaved very well, keeping up a constant retreating fire from behind houses. We presently saw their main body formed; but, from their motions, they seemed undetermined how to act. Being hard pressed by our troops, who had already got possession of their artillery, they attempted to file off by a road on their right, leading to Princeton. But, perceiving their intention, I threw a body of troops in their way, which immediately checked them. Finding from our disposition, that they were surrounded, and that they must inevitably be cut to pieces if they made any further resistance, they agreed to lay down their arms. The number that submitted in this manner was twenty-three officers and eight hundred and eighty six men. Colonel Rahl, the commanding officer, and seven others were found wounded in the town. I do not exactly know how many were killed; but I fancy twenty or thirty, as they never made any regular stand. Our loss is very trifling indeed, only two officers and one or two privates wounded.

In justice to the officers and men, I must add, that their behavior upon this occasion reflects the highest honor upon them. The difficulty of passing the river in a very severe night, and their march through a violent storm of snow and hail, did not in the least abate their ardor; but, when they came to the charge, each seemed to vie with the other in pressing forward; and were I to give a preference to any particular corps, I should do great injustice to the others.

George Washington, Report to John Hancock on the victory at Trenton, December 1776, in John C. Fitzpatrick, ed., *The Writings of George Washington, from the Original Manuscript Sources, 1745–1799.* 39 vols. Washington, D.C.: United States Government Printing Office, 1931–1944.

A Close Call for General Washington

In July 1777 General Howe put into motion his scheme of capturing Philadelphia, the seat of the Continental Congress. Howe sailed with thirteen thousand men from New York and went first to New Jersey, where he performed some useless maneuvers before setting sail again for Pennsylvania. The time in New Jersey delayed his approach to Philadelphia for two months. On September 11 Howe was finally on the road to Philadelphia when he met part of George Washington's army at Brandywine Creek.

The Battle of Brandywine was a heated affair. Washington had poor intelligence of the enemy, however, and when he sent part of his reserve forces to aid units engaged with Howe's Hessian mercenaries, he had no idea that a British column under Lord Cornwallis had maneuvered to his rear. Cornwallis surprised the Americans and forced them into retreat. With

The Battle of Brandywine. Although the Americans suffered many casualties, General William Howe was unable to destroy Washington's army.

his army split, Washington called a general with-drawal to avert a disaster. By nightfall the Americans had escaped the British trap and retired from the fight. The British were too tired and disorganized to pursue. Though they failed again to crush Washington's army, the British did inflict around fourteen hundred casualties on the Americans, and the way was open to Philadelphia.

Major Patrick Ferguson was a British officer who raised a unit of Tory volunteers in America to scout and fight for the Crown. He was also renowned for inventing the breech-loading rifle, a weapon that could be charged and fired faster than the standard-issue muzzle-loaded musket. At Brandywine, Ferguson's volunteers employed their breech-loaders to great effect. And it was in this battle that Ferguson claims he almost changed the course of the war. Ferguson was on a scouting mission while attached to the Hessian regiments. By his own account, written into a biography by James Ferguson, he and his fellow scouts saw two horsemen approach his concealed location. Ferguson recognized one as a colonial officer. He issued the order to fire but then rescinded out of some unexplained sense of chivalry. Only later did Ferguson discover the identity of the colonial officer.

Patrick Ferguson, scouting ahead of his men when the sound of horses' hoof beats drove him to take cover. He had the chance of ending the life of the enemy commander or perhaps of the war. In the battle itself, Ferguson's right elbow was to be shattered.

"We had not lain long . . . when a rebel officer, remarkable by a hussar dress, passed towards our army within a hundred yards of my right flank, not perceiving us. He was followed by another dressed in dark green or blue, mounted on a bay horse, with a remarkably large cocked hat.

"I ordered three good shots to steal near . . . and fire at them, but the idea disgusted me. I recalled the order. The hussar in returning made a circuit, but the other passed again within a hundred yards of us, upon which I advanced from the woods towards him.

"On my calling, he stopped, but after looking at me, proceeded. I again drew his attention and made signs to stop but he slowly continued his way. As I was within that distance at which in the quickest firing I could have lodged half-a-dozen of balls in or about him before he was out of my reach, I had only to determine. But it was not pleasant to fire at the back of an unoffending individual, who was acquitting himself very coolly of his duty, so I let him alone.

"The day after, I had been telling this story to some wounded officers who lay in the same room with me, when one of our surgeons, who had been dressing the wounded rebel officers, came in and told us they had been informing him that General Washington was all the morning with the light troops and only attended by a French Officer in a hussar dress, he himself dressed and mounted in every point as above described. I am not sorry that I did not know at the time who it was."

James Ferguson, *Two Scottish Soldiers, A Soldier of 1688 and Blenheim, A Soldier of the American Revolution, and a Jacobite Laird and His Forebears.* Aberdeen, Scotland: D. Wyllie & Sons, 1888.

Losses at Germantown

After successfully capturing Philadelphia, General William Howe divided his forces, stationing some in the city and sending others across the Delaware River to neighboring Germantown, Pennsylvania. George Washington hoped to take advantage of Howe's decision and planned a surprise raid on the nine thousand British troops holding Germantown on October 4, 1777. Washington's strategy involved bringing four columns of men together— two of well-trained Continental regulars and two of colonial militia—to have enough strength to deal a decisive blow to the British. Although the plan sounded good, it fell apart in execution. The two militia units never arrived at Germantown, and the two columns of regulars—one under the command of General Nathanael Greene and the other led by General John Sullivan—came together and mistook each other for the enemy. They opened fire, killing and wounding several of their own compatriots.

When the colonials finally reorganized, they succeeded in catching Howe's men unprepared, but they could not coordinate their movements and attacks very well. The British, however, called on their expert training and quickly dominated the battlefield. After three hours of fighting, each side lost about five hundred men as casualties, but the colonials had another four hundred captured in the confusing fray. Washington withdrew with little to show for his surprise attack.

In the days that followed, colonial newspapers tried to turn Washington's defeat at Germantown into a strategic victory. Some claimed Washington's withdrawal was a planned event

Troops under the command of General Nathanael Greene (left) and General John Sullivan (right) mistook each other for the enemy at Germantown.

to distract the British, who were bent on grabbing nearby stores of colonial weapons and ammunition. Others simply argued that though Philadelphia was still in British hands, the colonial forces remained dominant in the region. The following letter, dated October 8, appeared in the Virginia Gazette *on October 18. It exemplifies the type of pro-colonial propaganda that exaggerated British losses and colonial bravery at Germantown.*

Our loss is pretty well fixed to seven hundred killed, wounded, and missing; that of the enemy not certainly known, but surely very great, as you may judge by the following intelligence, brought this evening by General Green's aid de camp, and which he says may be relied upon: General Agnew, Colonels Walcot, Abercrombie, and Thomas Byrd, from Virginia, with General De Heister's son, killed; General Kniphaufen wounded in the hand; and between two and three hundred wagons, loaded with wounded, sent into Philadelphia. That General Howe had sent about two thousand Hessians over Schuylkill (denoting a retreat) and that he had refused to let any of the inhabitants of Philadelphia go to see the field of battle".

"General Schuyler writes us, the twenty ninth of September, that if superior numbers, health, and spirits, can give success, our army in the Northern department will have it this campaign.

"For my part, I do not despair of success in this quarter also. Another such battle as the last will totally unfit General Howe for pursuing farther hostilities this campaign, and again possess us of Philadelphia."

This moment an express arrived, with a letter from Capt. William Pierce, dated Skippack camp, 12 o'clock P. M. the day on which the above bloody battle was fought. It contains sundry particulars, but the printer has only time to relate the following, viz. Our glorious general, after an animating speech to his army, directed them to hold themselves in readiness to march at 6 o'clock, with two days provision, ordered large fires to be made in the camp, and the tents to stand till nine at night, when they were to be struck, and put into the baggage wagons. The army marched all night, arrived at Chestnut Hill about day-break, and immediately fell upon the enemy's picket guard, with such fury and firmness, that they were instantly routed, with great laughter.

The whole army then pushed towards Germantown, but were met by the main body of the British army consisting of about ten thousand men, when a hot and dreadful engagement ensued. After an incessant fire of cannon and musketry, for upwards of an hour, the enemy gave way in all quarters, and our men drove them, with fixed bayonets, for near two miles, when they formed again. Our men with readiness and intrepidity, broke them a second time, and they retreated in great disorder to Germantown, with our whole army in close pursuit of them, till they got about halfway the town, when they took to the houses, and opened upon our men two or three field pieces with grape shot, which played with such violence that general Sullivan's division gave way, and we, in turn, were beat back better than two miles. Both armies, being greatly fatigued, shewed a willingness to discontinue the fight, and ours were ordered to march to Skippack creek, where they are now encamped. The enemy contented themselves with their last advantage, and retired to their old quarters at Germantown. They must have had 1000 killed dead on the field, and at least 1500 wounded. A Captain, and twenty five men, fell into our hands. Our loss does not exceed three hundred killed, and five hundred wounded. We brought off two field pieces, and two wagons loaded with baggage. General Nash is mortally wounded with a cannon ball. Col. Hendricks is wounded below the left eye, but likely to recover; he behaved with such heroism, that he was the admiration of the field. Lieut. Col. Parker, of the second Virginia regiment, a brave officer, got wounded in the leg, and it is said the bone is broke. Col. Matthew Smith, our deputy adjutant general, got his leg broke by a grape shot. Cornet Baylor, of the light horse, had one half of his foot shot away. Major Jameson had his horse killed under him, but he himself was unhurt. Capt. Dickinson was slightly wounded in the knee. Capt. Thomas Edmonds was so badly wounded, that he died in a few hours. Capt. Eustace, of the first Virginia regiment, was killed dead on the spot. Two Maryland colonels, of the name of Stone, were wounded, and many other officers, that I cannot recollect at present. The heroism and gallantry of the second Virginia regiment I cannot help particularly mentioning; they would do honour to any country in the world. It is universally believed they behaved the best of any troops in the field.

Excerpt from a report on American losses at Germantown, *Virginia Gazette*, October 18, 1777.

Serving with the Americans

Just after the Revolutionary War began, America was in need of a foreign ally. It logically looked to France, the age-old rival of England. France was keen on aiding the rebellion, but it was not immediately willing to declare war on England. After all, the revolution could fail, and France had many colonies in North America that it was not willing to lose to the large number of British troops already stationed there. Still, the French sent secret stores of munitions and money to the young American government. Perhaps more importantly, though, many French military officers volunteered to help train the Continental army. The most notable was the young Marquis de Lafayette, who obtained the rank of major general in American service.

Over the course of the war, other foreign governments sent military advisers to the colonies. Some were drawn by the ideas of liberty and freedom expressed by Thomas Paine and Thomas Jefferson. Others were influenced by Washington's victory at Trenton and even his bold ac-

The Marquis de Lafayette found the Continental army untrained, unskilled, and poorly equipped.

tions at Germantown. The "army" they found in America, however, was nothing like the ones they had left in Europe. The colonials had spirit, but they lacked standard-issue uniforms and weapons, and they had no knowledge of battlefield tactics. In the following letter, a French officer who accompanied the Americans in the battles around Philadelphia in 1777 describes the advantages and disadvantages of the colonial forces. Of prime concern in his assessment is the Americans' inability to stand up to the ferocious British bayonet charge. The officer concludes that without bayonets of their own—and the training to use them properly—the Continentals will likely continue to flee before the well-executed British charge.

If General Howe does not take care, he may find himself made very uneasy, even in his camp at Germantown, by the Americans; and if one of their divisions . . . gone astray in the woods . . . had not been two hours late, the English would have been repulsed as far as Philadelphia and perhaps farther. There was a very thick mist, and still these folks are so little warlike! But they are beginning to get used to fire. Without all these obstacles, Howe would have been cut to pieces. He has beaten these folks in two spirited battles since he landed in Chesapeake Bay. Let him look out for a third battle! He buys them by dint of men, and it is not so easy for him to recruit his army as it is for these folks who have plenty of militia and resources.

But the principal advantage of General Howe's army over General Washington's in the two battles fought by them, must be ascribed to their being more trained to the use of the bayonet. The American army know their superior dexterity in firing well, and rely entirely upon it. The British Army know it likewise, and dread it. Hence in all engagements the British soldiers rush on with the bayonet after one fire, and seldom fail of throwing the Americans into confusion. Habit, which forms men to do anything, I am persuaded would soon render these brave people as firm at the approaches of a bayonet, as the whistling of a musket ball. General [Charles] Lee, I am told, took great pains to eradicate the universal prejudice he found among the Americans, in favor of terminating the war with fire arms alone. "We must learn to face our enemies," said he, "man to man in the open field, or we shall never beat them." The late General [Richard] Montgomery, who served his apprenticeship in the British Army, knew so well that nothing but the bayonet would ever rout troops that had been trained to it, that he once proposed in the Convention of New York, of which he was a member, that directions should be given, both in Europe and in this country, to make all muskets intended for the American soldiers two inches longer than the muskets now in use in the British Army, in order that they may have an advantage of their enemy, in charge with bayonets, for, he said, "Britain will never yield but to the push of the bayonet."

Anonymous French officer, letter regarding his service with the Americans, ca. 1777.

A Loyalist Newspaper Report

Although the Revolutionary War is often thought of as a contest between England and America, it was also a civil war that pitted American against American. The colonies were not entirely inhabited by patriots who were eager to throw off British rule; there were many loyal supporters of the Crown who felt that the rebellion was nothing more than treason. As patriot factions—known commonly by the political name of Whigs—banded together to harass loyalists, so, too, did Crown supporters—known as Tories—gather in strength to defend themselves.

Some Tories fled to England when hostilities became intense; others formed militia units to fight alongside the British.

James Rivington was a newspaper publisher in New York whose loyalty to England obliged him to flee the city when Washington's army arrived. After General William Howe captured New York, Rivington was able to return. He reestablished his New York Loyal Gazette *in October 1777 and began printing once again. In his first editorial after the unplanned hiatus, Rivington speaks of the time when his newspaper was shut down by the Whigs. Ironically reflecting patriot complaints of abuses suffered at the hands of the Crown, Rivington asserts that he and others who remain loyal to England have been unjustly treated by tyrannical rebels who ignore laws and confiscate property at will.*

The Printer of this Paper, being again happily arrived in this City, presents his most respectful Compliments to the Public in general, and to his former Subscribers in particular. — He assures them, he entertains the most grateful Sense of the kind Support which they formerly afforded his Newspaper, and which they had Firmness enough to continue through a long Period of Confusion, Anarchy, and Tyranny; till an armed Banditti from Connecticut, in open Defiance of all Law, and in direct Violation of the sacred Rights of Humanity, forcibly entered his House at Noon Day, and robbed him of his Types and other Property to a considerable Amount: The Suppression of his Paper was the necessary Consequence, and the unremitted Perse-

Angry patriots walk through town with a loyalist captive.

cution of the said bitter Party obliged him to abandon his Dwelling in this City, and seek an Asylum in England, till by the Interposition of Government, some good Security for his Liberty and Property could be obtained. When he first began to publish a Weekly Paper, he is conscious to himself that he set out with the most upright Intentions. And when the Rebellion, which is now increased to so alarming an Height, began to open, it was his Ambition to make his Paper and Press as extensively and highly useful to this Country as possible, by printing such detached Pieces and Pamphlets as had a Tendency to preserve Peace, Order, and legal Government; to keep up and strengthen our Connection with the Mother Country, and to promote

a proper Subordination to the Supreme Authority of the British Empire. He flatters himself that his Endeavours in these Respects were not unacceptable to the loyal Part of the People in this Country, nor entirely without Effect.

Upon the same Principles he now begs Leave again to solicit the Favour of his former Friends, of those Gentlemen who have lately come to reside in this City, and of the Public in general. He assures them that Truth, Candour, and Decorum, shall ever preside over his Press. And, as it will be his constant Endeavour, he thinks he can take upon him to engage, that the Quality and Quantity of Intelligence, and other literary Matter in his Paper, will be such as shall give general Satisfaction to those who may be pleased to encourage it.

The happy Prospect now opening to us from the great Success with which it hath pleased God to bless his Majesty's Arms, both in the southern and northern Departments, must fill every loyal Heart with unfeigned Joy. Supremely happy will the Printer be, if he can make his Paper subservient to the Intentions of Government, — the Restoration of Peace, Order, and Happiness through the Continent, — by recalling the infatuated Multitude to the Use of their Reason and Understanding, and by convincing them how grossly they have been imposed upon by the Misrepresentations and false Glosses of their Leaders in Sedition and Rebellion.

James Rivington, *New York Loyal Gazette*, October 11, 1777.

General Horatio Gates prevented General John Burgoyne from taking Saratoga.

The Turning Point at Saratoga

While General William Howe conducted his Philadelphia campaign against George Washington, General John Burgoyne led an expedition from Canada to seize the Hudson River valley. In June 1777 he set out on a long trek with the intention of reaching Albany, New York. American militia and Continental regulars met him at every stage of his progress southward. Burgoyne was able to overcome the rebels and seize several important forts along the route, but each battle drained him of men and supplies. Meanwhile, the delays allowed more colonial forces to gather.

Burgoyne's successes, however, prompted the Continental Congress to promote Horatio Gates to overall command of the colonial units in the region on August 19. The promotion was pri-

marily a diplomatic gesture since Gates, a New Englander, was thought to possess the loyalty of the New England militiamen who were now fighting for their homes. Gates was determined to keep Burgoyne from reaching his objective. As Burgoyne crossed the Hudson River with his six thousand men—who by now were in desperate need of resupply—Gates had his men positioned behind fortifications on Bemis Heights, a few miles north of Saratoga, New York, awaiting the British advance.

Burgoyne pushed into the weak American left flank at a place called Freeman's Farm on September 19. Benedict Arnold, a subordinate American commander foresaw the danger and rallied troops to stem the British attack. Arnold's move saved the flank and delivered a smashing blow to Burgoyne. Hessian troops came to Burgoyne's aid and eventually held back Arnold's advance. Still, the British lost about six hundred men in the fray, compared to the three hundred colonial casualties. In the following letter John Glover, a colonial participant in the Battle of Freeman's Farm, relates to a relative the effect the losses had on both the colonial and British armies.

Glover's letter is dated September 29. Eight days later, Burgoyne would again try to break the colonial lines on Bemis Heights. Gates predicted the move and launched an attack to coincide with the British advance. The colonials, who outnumbered the British almost four to one, repeatedly broke the British lines. Soon after, Burgoyne tried to retreat across the Hudson. His path was blocked by colonials who had out-

flanked him. With hungry, demoralized men—many of whom were wounded—General Burgoyne surrendered his army on October 17. The victory had tremendous significance. Gates had not only won the Saratoga campaign, but he had also forced the surrender of an entire British army. This was a feat George Washington had yet to accomplish. Gates achieved instant recognition as "the Hero of Saratoga," and colonial spirits ran high. Perhaps more importantly, foreign powers like France and Spain took notice of the victory and began to consider seriously the notion of formally allying with the rebel government.

British and American soldiers meet in the Battle of Freeman's Farm.

DEAR SIRS:

Since my last letter to you we have had two flags of truce from the enemy, by which we have received an account of their killed and wounded in the battle of the 19th, 746, among which is a great proportion of officers. But the truth has not come out yet, as I'm fully persuaded, & it's the opinion of all the Gen. Officers, that they must have suffered a great many more.

We had 20 taken prisoners, of which seven were wounded. Gen. Burgoyne sent a return of their names by the flag, with a very polite letter to Gen. Gates, who returned as polite a one, with a list of 70 prisoners, 30 odd of which were wounded. These I think will ballance the 20.

We had 81 officers and men killed dead on the spot and 202 wounded, many of which are since dead, in the whole 303—a very inconsiderable number, when we consider how hot the battle was & how long it continued, being 6 hours without any intermission, saving about half an hour between 2 and 3 o'clock.

The enemy have remained very quiet ever since at about one mile distance, not attempting to advance one step. We are continually harrassing them by driving their pickets, bringing off their horses &c.

We have taken 30 prisoners since the battle, and as many more deserted.

Our men are in fine spirits, are very bold and daring, a proof of which I will give you in an instance two nights past.

I ordered 100 men from my Brigade to take off a picket of about 60 of the enemy, who were posted about half a mile from me, at the same time ordered a covering party of 200 to support them. This being the first enterprise of this kind, & as it was proposed by me, I was very anxious for its success. I therefore went myself. The night being very foggy and dark, could not find the enemy till after day. When I made the proper disposition for the attack, they went on like so many tigers, bidding defiance to musket balls and bayonets. Drove the enemy, killed 3, and wounded a great number more, took one prisoner, 8 Packs, 8 Blankets, 2 guns, 1 sword, and many other articles of Plunder without any loss on our side.

Matters can't remain long as they now are. Burgoyne has only 20 days provision. He must give us battle in a day or two, or else retire back.

The latter I think he'll endeavor to do; in either case I think, with the blessing of Heaven he must be ruined.

We are now between 10 & 11000, strong, healthy and in fine fighting cue, I am fully satisfied they will fight hard, when called to action. God grant that every man may do his duty, and be crowned with success, which will put an end to our trouble in this quarter; at least this campaign, and I am inclined to think forever. My compliments to your good ladies, families and all friends, and believe me to be respectfully,

yr friend & most obedt. servt.,

N. B. This moment 4 Hessian deserters came in who say that 1/2 the company agreed to come off with them, & that we may expect a great many more very soon.

John Glover, "Letter to Jonathan Glover and Azor Orne, September 29, 1777," in *Historical Collections of the Essex Institute*, vol. 5. Salem, MA: G.M. Whipple & A.A. Smith, 1863.

Prisoners in Boston

When General John Burgoyne surrendered his army at the Battle of Saratoga, the German mercenaries in his command also became colonial prisoners. Baron von Riedesel, a major general, was one of the captured. He and his wife joined many other prisoners of war detained in Boston. Frederika von Riedesel recorded the treatment she and her small entourage received in the city gripped by patriotic fervor.

*Eighteenth-century military protocol stipu-
lated that officers captured in battle were to be
well treated; in return, they were bound by a
code of honor not to flee from captivity. Typically, captured troops were not held for long and
were eventually returned to their homelands
with the pledge that they could not return to
fight in the war. Considering this prevailing
chivalrous attitude, the baroness's "sufferings"
may seem mild by modern standards.*

We finally reached Boston, and our troops
were quartered in barracks not far away,
on Winter Hill. We were put up at a
farmer's house, where we were given only
one room in the attic. My maids slept on
the floor, and the men in the hall. Some
straw on which I had spread our bedding
was all we had for a long while on which to
sleep, since I had nothing other than my
field bed. Our host allowed us to eat downstairs in his room, where his whole family
ate and slept together. The man was good,
but his wife, in revenge for the bother we
caused her, deliberately chose to vex us
during our mealtime by combing her children's hair, which was full of vermin, often
making us lose every bit of appetite, and
when we asked her to do her combing outside, or at some other time, she replied, "It
is my room; I see fit to stay and to comb my
children now." We had to hold our silence,
for otherwise she might have turned us
out of the house.

One day, our gentlemen, disregarding
this filth, celebrated the birthday, I believe,
of the Queen of England, by drinking a
good deal of wine. My two elder daughters, little Augusta and Frederika, having
noticed that the wine left over had been
stowed away under the stairs, helped themselves to some of it so that they could also
drink to the Queen's health. They sat outside by the door and drank so many toasts
that their little heads could stand no more
and Frederika even developed a fever,
which frightened me terribly, because she
had cramps, and I could not possibly think
what had caused them. When nature finally came to aid by causing her to vomit,
I saw the whole trouble came from wine
and scolded the little girls severely, whereupon they replied that they also loved the
King and the Queen and, therefore, could
not refrain from wishing them happiness.

We stayed in this place three weeks before we were then taken to Cambridge,
where we were put up in one of the most
beautiful houses, previously the property
of royalists [i.e., loyalists]. I have never
seen a lovelier location. Seven families,
partly relatives and partly friends, had
leasehold estates here with gardens and
magnificent houses and orchards nearby.
All these estates were only about an eighth
of a mile apart from one another. The
owners gathered every afternoon at one of
the homes or another, where they enjoyed
themselves with music and dancing, living
happily in comfort and harmony until,
alas, the devastating war separated them
all, leaving all the houses desolate with the
exception of two, whose owners shortly
thereafter were also obliged to flee.

None of our gentlemen were permitted to go to Boston. My curiosity and the desire to see [colonial] General [Philip] Schuyler's daughter, Mrs. Carter, impelled me to go, and I had dinner with her there several times. It is quite a pretty city, but inhabited by enthusiastic patriots and full of wicked people; the women, particularly, were horrid, casting ugly looks at me, and some of them even spitting when I passed by them. Mrs. Carter was gentle and good, like her parents, but her husband was a bad and treacherous person. They often visited us and ate with us and the other generals. We did our utmost to reciprocate their kindness. They seemed to feel very friendly toward us too, but it was during this time that this horrible Mr. Carter made the gruesome suggestion to the Americans, when the English General Howe had set fire to many villages and towns, to behead our generals, put the heads in small barrels, salt them, and send one of these barrels to the English for each village or town which they had set on fire. This beastly suggestion fortunately, however, was not adopted.

While in England I had become acquainted with a Captain Fenton of Boston, whose services the Americans had wanted when the war broke out, but who, being faithful to his King, had refused to obey. Hereupon the women among the embittered mob grabbed his wife, a most respectable lady, and his pretty fifteen-year-old daughter, and disregarding their goodness, beauty, and embarrassment, un-dressed them to the skin, tarred and feathered them, and paraded them through the city. What may one not expect from people of this sort, animated by the most bitter hate! . . .

On June 3, 1778, I gave a ball and supper in celebration of my husband's birthday. I had invited all the generals and officers. The Carters also came, but General Burgoyne sent his apologies after having kept us waiting until eight o'clock in the evening. On one pretext or another he refused every invitation of ours until he left for England. Before his departure he called on me to make his apologies personally, to which I merely replied that I should have been sorry if he had put himself to any inconvenience for our sake. There was much dancing, and my cook had prepared an excellent supper for more than eighty guests. Moreover, our court and the garden were illuminated. As the King's birthday was on the 4th, the day after, we decided not to part until we could drink to the King's health, which was done with the most sincere loyalty, both toward his person and toward his cause.

Never, I believe, was "God save the King" sung with more enthusiasm or greater sincerity. Even my two elder daughters were brought downstairs to join us and see the illumination. All eyes were filled with tears, and everyone seemed proud of having the courage to celebrate thus in the midst of the enemy. Even the Carters had not the heart to hold themselves aloof. When the company left, we saw that the house was entirely surrounded by Americans, who, upon seeing so many people enter and observing the illumination, had grown suspicious, fearing that we were planning a revolt, and had there been the slightest noise, we should have had to pay dearly for it. . . .

My husband frequently suffered from nervousness and depression. The only thing that helped him in this mood was to go walking, or to work in the garden, so whenever we were obliged to move, I always managed to have a garden prepared for him, which was no great difficulty and cost very little, because almost all our soldiers could do garden work and were glad to earn a bit extra. I thanked God more than ever that he had given me courage to join my husband! The misery of being kept a prisoner, the unfortunate position of our troops, and the lack of news from home all made my husband depressed. How much greater would his misery have been if he had had no one to divert his thoughts during the six months and more he would have been without news from us. How happy I am, even now, when I recollect those times, that I had paid no attention to the people who wanted to prevent me from doing my duty and following the call of my heart, and that I faithfully shared all his suffering and his sorrow.

Frederika von Riedesel, notes on her imprisonment in Boston.

Winter at Valley Forge

After the British captured Philadelphia, they engaged in a few skirmishes with George Washington's army but retired to the city to wait out the winter. Washington bottled up Philadelphia, but he could not lay an effective siege. He retired his army to winter quarters at Valley Forge, Pennsylvania. By the end of 1777 many of his militiamen had deserted him to return to their homes. The remnants braved freezing cold at a camp without adequate shelter or provisions. Many of the soldiers had worn through their shoes during months of marching and were forced to wrap their feet in linen to withstand the chill.

Many colonists returned home during the winter, but those who remained at Valley Forge suffered from lack of food and decent quarters.

Albigence Waldo was a colonial soldier in Washington's camp. In this excerpt from his diary, Waldo speaks of his own fatigue and sickness as well as the general suffering of all those who endured the bitterly cold months at Valley Forge.

December 14.—Prisoners & Deserters are continually coming in. The Army which has been surprisingly healthy hitherto, now begins to grow sickly from the continued fatigues they have suffered this Campaign. Yet they still show a spirit of Alacrity & Contentment not to be expected from so young Troops. I am Sick—discontented—and out of humour. Poor food—hard lodging—Cold Weather—fatigue—Nasty Cloaths—nasty Cookery—Vomit half my time—smoak'd out of my senses—the Devil's in't—I can't Endure it—Why are we sent here to starve and Freeze—What sweet Felicities have I left at home; A charming Wife—pretty Children—Good Beds—good food—good Cookery—all agreeable—all harmonious. Here all Confusion—smoke & Cold—hunger & filthyness—A pox on my bad luck. There comes a bowl of beef soup—full of burnt leaves and dirt, sickish enough to make a Hector spue—away with it Boys—I'll live like the Chameleon upon Air. Poh! Poh! crys Patience within me—you talk like a fool. Your being sick Covers your mind with a Melanchollic Gloom, which makes every thing about you appear gloomy. See the poor Soldier, when in health—with what cheerfulness he meets his foes and encounters every hardship—if barefoot, he labours thro' the Mud & Cold with a Song in his mouth extolling War & Washington—if his food be bad, he eats it notwithstanding with seeming content—blesses God for a good Stomach and Whistles it into digestion. But harkee Patience, a moment—There comes a Soldier, his bare feet are seen thro' his worn out Shoes, his legs nearly naked from the tatter'd remains of an only pair of stockings, his Breeches not sufficient to cover his nakedness, his Shirt hanging in Strings, his hair dishevell'd, his face meagre; his whole appearance pictures a person forsaken & discouraged. He comes, and crys with an air of wretchedness & despair, I am Sick, my feet lame, my legs are sore, my body cover'd with this tormenting Itch—my Cloaths are worn out, my Constitution is broken, my former Activity is exhausted by fatigue, hunger & Cold, I fail fast I shall soon be no more! and all the reward I shall get will be—"Poor Will is dead." People who live at home in Luxury and Ease, quietly possessing their habitations, Enjoying their Wives & families in peace, have but a very faint Idea of the unpleasing sensations, and continual Anxiety the Man endures who is in a Camp, and is the husband and parent of an agreeable family. These same People are willing we should suffer every thing for their Benefit & advantage, and yet are the first to Condemn us for not doing more!!

Albigence Waldo, "Diary entry, December 14, 1777," in *Pennsylvania Magazine of History and Biography*, vol. 21. Philadelphia: Historical Society of Pennsylvania, 1897.

Chapter 5

On to Yorktown

In early 1778 another colonial delegation that included the venerable Benjamin Franklin met with King Louis XVI. The French monarch agreed to officially commit his nation and its military to the cause of American liberty. In February the treaty was signed. When news reached the colonies, the Continental army was elated. France would provide veteran soldiers to help fight land battles, but more importantly, the French naval fleet would contest the superiority that the British navy had enjoyed for the past three years (and utilized so effectively in England's coastal campaigns against Boston and New York). George Washington was particularly pleased with the French commitment. He hoped the assistance would enable him to take the war to the British instead of having to fight on the defensive so often. He understood that another major defeat of a British army might persuade Britain's Parliament to quit the war since the fighting was both draining England's finances and

becoming more and more unpopular with the British public. But he also realized that the French mobilization would take time, and that until France could send troops across the Atlantic, America was on its own in keeping up the fight.

As the year 1778 dawned in the British camp, General William Howe resigned his command of the Crown forces in America. Howe had grown tired of the war, and his reputation was tarnishing in England because he had not yet achieved a decisive victory against General Washington. No British successor volunteered to take command, so the appointment fell to a reluctant Henry Clinton. The first order the new commander received was to evacuate Philadelphia and return with part of his command to New York. The rest of his army was sent to Florida and the West Indies to protect British interests in anticipation of France's entry into the war.

The bulk of the British forces remained in New York for the next two years

General Henry Clinton succeeded General William Howe as commander of British forces in America.

with Washington's army camped on the city's outskirts. Clinton, however, sailed a sizable part of the army down to the southern colonies to strike Georgia and the Carolinas. Fearing the British reserves in New York would run rampant through New England if left unguarded, Washington decided he could not afford to abandon his positions around New York to counter the attacks in the South. Instead, he sent General Benjamin Lincoln with a small number of troops to Charleston, South Carolina, in the hopes that the strategic port city could be saved. Lincoln was capable, but his lack of manpower proved too much of a handicap. On May 12, 1780, the city fell. Leaving Charles Cornwallis in charge of roughly eight thousand British

troops and colonial loyalists in the South to safeguard the region, Clinton sailed back to New York.

Lord Cornwallis was an ambitious general who believed the Revolutionary War could be won in the southern colonies. General Clinton disagreed; he believed the next major colonial offensive would come in the North, and he was unwilling to support Cornwallis's plan to eradicate southern resistance. Clinton wanted Cornwallis's army ready to assist New York when Washington decided to move. But in the early months of 1781, against Clinton's wishes, Lord Cornwallis went venturing through Virginia attacking American outposts without achieving any significant victories. Clinton tolerated the move, anticipating that from Virginia, Cornwallis would be even closer when assistance was needed. He ordered Cornwallis to return to the Virginia coast and wait for orders. Cornwallis complied and set up camp at Yorktown, a few miles from the colonial capital at Williamsburg.

Meanwhile, George Washington was indeed thinking of attacking in the North, but his plan was happily derailed. A French general, the Comte de Rochambeau, had arrived in Rhode Island with five thousand French soldiers early in 1781. Rochambeau favored making a strong, coordinated attack in the South because a French naval fleet under the Comte de Grasse was sailing up the Atlantic seaboard from the West Indies and could help in an assault against the unsuspecting Cornwallis. Washington agreed to the bold plan. Leaving a token force behind in New York so as not to alert Clinton to the plan, Washington and Rochambeau moved their armies to Virginia.

In September 1781 the French fleet bottled up the Chesapeake Bay and fought off an English squadron of ships, depriving Cornwallis of naval assistance and leaving his army no escape route by sea. Then nearly nine thousand colonials and eight thousand French troops encircled Cornwallis's seven thousand men at Yorktown. Over the last weeks of September and the early weeks of October, the French and Americans laid siege to the entrenchments

The Comte de Rochambeau arrived with his soldiers and ships to help fight General Charles Cornwallis and his army.

Cornwallis had dug around the town. Cornwallis sent word to Clinton of his predicament. Clinton replied that he would organize a relief force to sail to Cornwallis's rescue. But the English fleet needed favorable winds, which were not forthcoming. By October 17 Cornwallis's defenses had been overrun and he had a town full of dead and wounded. He surrendered by midmorning on the fourth anniversary of General Burgoyne's surrender at Saratoga.

In a practical sense, the successful campaign at Yorktown ended the war. Sir Guy Carleton replaced Clinton as the commander of England's forces in the colonies, and Carleton's first measure was to negotiate a cease-fire with George Washington. Although some skirmishes continued between loyalists and colonials in the backcountry of the South and around the Ohio River valley, no major engagements took place for the last two years of the war. King George was eager to continue the fight, but the English people had had enough. The pro-war government fell, and Parliament worked to hammer out a treaty with the colonials. On September 3, 1783, the Treaty of Paris left England its holdings in Canada and the West Indies, but the former colonies in America—now united—were given their independence. After an eight-year war, America was finally a free, sovereign nation.

Forging an Alliance with France

To secure its independence, America needed the aid of foreign powers. France was the nation most willing to help the revolutionaries, primarily because France and England had been rivals for many years. In 1776 France began covertly sending arms, munitions, and money to the colonies. Two years later the Continental Congress sent an official delegation to the court of King Louis XVI to negotiate a formal treaty with France. Seventy-year-old Benjamin Franklin was one of three men assigned to this diplomatic mission.

Benjamin Franklin bows before King Louis XVI on a diplomatic visit. As ambassador, he negotiated a peace treaty with France.

The French adored Franklin because of his scholarship and Enlightenment ideals. He was instrumental in garnering the Treaty of Amity and Commerce and a mutual defense agreement that cemented the international relationship and brought French military forces into the war against England. Although America already had the help of French officers who had volunteered to serve in the Continental army, the rebellion now gained the might of the French fleet, a force to counter the as-yet-unchallenged British navy, which had swayed many Revolutionary battles in Britain's favor.

In the following letter to Continental Congressman Thomas Cushing, Benjamin Franklin speaks of his delegation's success in securing the commercial and military treaties with France in February 1778. He lists some of the provisions of the treaties, and he mentions that the pact is to be kept secret for a short time—actually until the French fleet could sail to American waters and not be stopped along the way by the British. Finally, Franklin acknowledges that Spain was expected to offer its formal support to the colonial cause as well. Indeed, Spain had, like France, been supplying the rebellion with money for a few years. But Spain's king was not willing to formalize a treaty with America because he feared that if the rebellion failed, Spain could lose valuable holdings in North America. Instead, Spain's King Charles III went only as far as making an alliance with France to support its new fight against England.

I received your favor by Mr. Austin, with your most agreeable congratulations on the success of the American arms in the

Northern Department. In return, give me leave to congratulate you on the success of our negotiations here, in the completion of the two treaties with his most Christian Majesty: the one of amity and commerce, on the plan of that proposed by Congress, with some good additions; the other of alliance for mutual defence, in which the most Christian king agrees to make a common cause with the United States, if England attempts to obstruct the commerce of his subjects with them; and guarantees to the United States their liberty, sovereignty, and independence, absolute and unlimited, with all the possessions they now have, or may have, at the conclusion of the war; and the States in return guarantee to him his possessions in the West Indies. The great principle in both treaties is a perfect equality and reciprocity; no advantage to be demanded by France, or privileges in commerce, which the States may not grant to any and every other nation.

In short, the king has treated with us generously and magnanimously; taken no advantage of our present difficulties, to exact terms which we would not willingly grant, when established in prosperity and power. I may add that he has acted wisely, in wishing the friendship contracted by these treaties may be durable, which probably might not be if a contrary conduct had taken place.

Several of the American ships, with stores for the Congress, are now about sailing under the convoy of a French squadron. England is in great consternation, and the minister, on the 17th instant, confessing that all his measures had been wrong and that peace was necessary, proposed two bills for quieting America; but they are full of artifice and deceit, and will, I am confident, be treated accordingly by our country.

I think you must have much satisfaction in so valuable a son, whom I wish safe back to you, and am, with great esteem, etc.,

B. FRANKLIN.

P.S.—The treaties were signed by the plenipotentiaries [those invested with full power] on both sides February 6th, but are still for some reasons kept secret, though soon to be published. It is understood that Spain will soon accede to the same. The treaties are forwarded to Congress by this conveyance.

Benjamin Franklin, letter to Thomas Cushing, 1778.

The *Bon Homme Richard* vs. the *Serapis*

Early during the Revolutionary War the Continental Congress had authorized the formation of a navy, primarily to protect coastal towns and waterways and to harass British merchant shipping. The colonial fleet grew to include fifty-two ships of various sizes, but the number and condition of the vessels made them little match for the huge men-of-war in the Royal navy. Still, the Americans did achieve some impressive victories over their foe.

Perhaps the most notable victory was that of Captain John Paul Jones in 1779. Jones had

Britain and America wage war in the Baltic Sea.

Dale, in command of a section of colonial cannon, heard Captain Pearson hail the Bon Homme Richard *and ask if the colonials had struck their colors—that is, run up their flag as a sign of surrender. As Dale recorded in his account of the battle, John Paul Jones is said to have given his famous reply, "I have not yet begun to fight."*

After four hours of fighting, the colonial sailors boarded the Serapis *and forced the British to surrender. The* Bon Homme Richard *was too badly damaged to maintain its seaworthiness, so Jones had his men transfer to the* Serapis *and sail for a French port. The* Bon Homme Richard *sank on September 25. Despite the loss of the victorious ship, the victory was applauded in America, and Britain was frightened into keeping more of its warships closer to home.*

been commissioned with a French cargo ship (obtained by Benjamin Franklin while negotiating with France) that was refitted with cannon and christened the Bon Homme Richard. *Unlike most captains, who preferred to patrol close to home, Jones used his new warship to pursue English merchant ships in the waters around Britain. On September 23 Jones was stalking a fleet of merchantmen heading toward England from the Baltic Sea. His prey eluded him, but a fighting escort ship turned to engage. Off Flamborough Head, the* Serapis, *commanded by Captain Richard Pearson, took on the* Bon Homme Richard. *Jones quickly learned that his larger caliber guns had a tendency to explode when fired, so he decided to sail in close and ram the British ship. The maneuver was a success, and the two ships fought a confusing, entangled melee. At one point Lieutenant Richard*

At about eight, being within hail, the *Serapis* demanded, 'What ship is that?'

He was answered, 'I can't hear what you say.'

Immediately after, the *Serapis* hailed again, 'What ship is that? Answer immediately, or I shall be under the necessity of firing into you.'

At this moment I received orders from Commodore Jones to commence the action with a broadside, which indeed appeared to be simultaneous on board both ships. Our position being to windward of the *Serapis* we passed ahead of her, and the *Serapis* coming up on our larboard quarter, the action commenced abreast of each other. The *Serapis* soon passed ahead of the *Bonhomme Richard,* and when he thought he had gained a distance sufficient to go down athwart the fore foot, to rake us, found he had not enough distance, and that the *Bonhomme Richard* would be aboard him, put his helm a-lee, which brought the two ships on a line, and the *Bonhomme Richard,* having head way, ran her bows into the stern of the *Serapis.*

We had remained in this situation but a few minutes when we were again hailed by the *Serapis,* 'Has your ship struck?'

Captain John Paul Jones devised impressive naval tactics that gave him the advantage over Britain.

To which Captain Jones answered, 'I have not yet begun to fight!'

As we were unable to bring a single gun to bear upon the *Serapis* our top-sails were backed, while those of the *Serapis* being filled, the ships separated. The *Serapis* bore short round upon her heel, and her jibboom ran into the mizen rigging of the *Bonhomme Richard.* In this situation the ships were made fast together with a hawser, the bowsprit of the *Serapis* to the mizen-mast of the *Bonhomme Richard,* and the action recommenced from the starboard sides of the two ships. With a view of separating the ships, the *Serapis* let go her anchor, which manoeuver brought her head and the stern of the *Bonhomme Richard* to the wind, while the ships lay closely pressed against each other. A novelty in naval combats was now presented to many witnesses, but to few admirers. The rammers were run into the respective ships to enable the men to load after the lower ports of the *Serapis* had been blown away, to make room for running out their guns, and in this situation the ships remained until between 10 and 11 o'clock PM, when the engagement terminated by the surrender of the *Serapis.*

From the commencement to the termination of the action there was not a man on board the *Bonhomme Richard* ignorant of the superiority of the *Serapis,* both in weight of metal and in the qualities of the crews. The crew of that ship was picked seamen, and the ship itself had been only a few months off the stocks, whereas the crew of the *Bonhomme Richard* consisted of part Americans, English and French, and a part of Maltese, Portuguese and Malays, these latter contributing by their want of naval skill and knowledge of the English language to depress rather than to elevate a just hope of success in a combat under such circumstances. Neither the consideration of the relative force of the ships, the fact of the blowing up of the gundeck above them by the bursting of two of the 18-pounders, nor the alarm that the ship was sinking, could depress the ardor or change the determination of the brave Captain Jones, his officers and men. Neither the repeated broadsides of the Alliance, given with the view of sinking or disabling the *Bonhomme Richard,* the frequent necessity of suspending the combat to extinguish the flames, which several times were within a few inches of the magazine, nor the liberation by the master-at-arms of nearly 500 prisoners, could change or weaken the purpose of the American commander. At the moment of the liberation of the prisoners, one of them, a commander of a 20-gun ship taken a few days before, passed through the ports on board the *Serapis* and informed Captain Pearson that if he would hold out only a little while longer, the ship alongside would either strike or sink, and that all the prisoners had been released to save their lives. The combat was accordingly continued with renewed ardor by the *Serapis.*

The fire from the tops of the *Bonhomme Richard* was conducted with so much skill and effect as to destroy ultimately every man who appeared upon the quarter deck of the *Serapis,* and induced her commander to order the survivors to go below. Not even under the shelter of the decks were they more secure. The powder-monkies of the *Serapis,* finding no officer to receive the 18-pound cartridges brought from the magazines, threw them on the main deck and went for more. These cartridges being scattered along the deck and numbers of them broken, it so happened that some of the hand-grenades thrown from the main-yard of the *Bonhomme Richard,* which was directly over the main-hatch of the *Serapis,* fell upon this powder and produced a most awful explosion. The effect was tremendous; more than twenty of the enemy were blown to pieces, and many stood with only the collars of their shirts upon their bodies. In less than an hour afterwards, the flag of England, which had been nailed to the mast of the *Serapis,* was struck by Captain Pearson's own hand, as none of his people would venture aloft on this duty; and this too when more than 1500 persons were witnessing the conflict, and the humiliating termination of it, from Scarborough and Flamborough Head.

Richard Dale in John Henry Sherburne, *Life and Character of the Chevalier John Paul Jones.* Washington, 1825.

No Need for French Assistance

When the alliance between America and France was formalized in 1778, the reaction in the colonies was mostly favorable. However, not all patriots approved of bringing a foreign power into a war for national independence. Major Samuel Shaw was one of the skeptics. In the following letter, written two years after the alliance was made, Shaw reluctantly agrees that the French navy will certainly bolster the weak American fleet, but he argues that the blood of American soldiers alone should buy the nation's freedom. Otherwise, Shaw fears that Americans will not feel the pride and honor of having won the right to rule themselves.

As an American citizen, I rejoice in the prospect of so speedy and, I hope, an effectual aid. But as a soldier, I am dissatisfied. How will it sound in history, that the United States of America could not, or rather would not, make an exertion, when the means were amply in their power, which might at once rid them of their enemies, and put them in possession of that liberty and safety, for which we have been so long contending. By Heavens! if our rulers had any modesty, they would blush at the idea of calling in foreign aid! 'tis really abominable, that we should send to France for soldiers, when there are so many sons of America idle. Such a step ought not (had these great men any sensibility) to have been taken until the strength of the country had been nearly exhausted, and our freedom tottering on the brink of ruin. Let us be indebted to France, Spain, or even the Devil himself, if he could furnish it, for a navy, because we cannot get one seasonably among our-

selves. But do let us, unless we are contented to be transmitted to posterity with disgrace, make an exertion of our own strength by land, and not owe our independence entirely to our allies.

Samuel Shaw, letter to John Lamb, July 12, 1780.

The Siege of Yorktown

Early in 1781 British general Charles Cornwallis had finished conducting raids in the Carolinas and had returned to Virginia to begin a campaign of eliminating resistance in the interior of that colony. His superior, Sir Henry Clinton, was not in favor of Cornwallis's plan. Clinton knew that Cornwallis could become cut off by rebel forces in the interior of the colony, and that he would not be able to come to Cornwallis's rescue. He therefore instructed his subordinate to return to the coast and wait. After a fruitless chase of colonial forces under the Marquis de Lafayette, Cornwallis obeyed Clinton's command and holed up in the town of Yorktown near Chesapeake Bay.

During the first few months of 1781 the Marquis de Lafayette, now supported by the army of Anthony Wayne, set up camp outside Yorktown to watch Cornwallis's movements and to report any findings to George Washington. Washington was in New England at the time, discussing a siege of New York (where Clinton's army was) with the Comte de Rochambeau, the commander of the recently arrived French army. It was during these talks that Washington learned that the French fleet under the Comte de Grasse would be in the region of Chesapeake Bay in September.

General Charles Cornwallis of Great Britain could not fend off colonial forces at Yorktown.

Acknowledging that the combined American and French forces in New York could probably not carry the city, Washington decided to secretly leave New York and sail down the Chesapeake River to lay siege to Yorktown. He hoped that with the majority of the colonial forces, the French army, and the French fleet bottling up the town, he might just trap Cornwallis.

Washington's maneuver worked flawlessly, and on September 26 he arrived at Yorktown and pushed colonial strength up to 8,850 men, supported by 7,800 French troops under Rochambeau. By then the French fleet had fought a duel with the British squadron in the bay and forced its retreat to New York, leaving Cornwallis's 7,400 men no route of escape by sea. The next day Washington's army encircled

the town. Afraid his army was spread too thin, Cornwallis evacuated his outer defensive perimeter and moved his troops closer to positions in town. Washington's men took the empty positions and began digging a series of trenches from them that zigzagged toward the British lines. When they got close enough, they would storm an enemy redoubt, or earthen fortification. The British responded by sending out units to fight off the diggers. The battle proceeded in this manner throughout the early weeks of October.

St. George Tucker was a colonial colonel who participated in the siege. In his journal, he wrote of the slow process of inching ahead through the series of entrenchments as the noose tightened around Cornwallis's army.

Thursday 11th. Last Evening and during the night the Cannonade & Bombardment from ours & the french Batteries [groupings of weapons situated for battle] were kept up with very little Intermission. Red hot Balls being fired at the Shipping from the french Battery over the Creek, the Charon a forty four Gun ship and another ship were set fire to & burnt during the night & a Brig in the morning met with the same Fate—Our Batteries have continued an incessant Firing during the whole Day—This Evening I walk'd down to the Trenches—The Enemy threw a few shells from five mortars which appear to be in the Battery in front of Secry Nelson's House, at the French Battery near the Clay Hill (a small distance from Pigeon Hill). Most of these burst in the Air at a considerable Height nor do I know whether any one of them fell into, or near the Battery. After this their shells were directed apparently towards the place where we this Evening begun to open our second paralel—One half of them at least burst in the Air; I do not know what Effect the remainder had—A few shot at the Interval of twenty or thirty minutes were all the Annoyance we recieved from their works during the Evening, except the Shells—I this day dined in Company with the Secretary. He says our Bombardment produced great Effects in annoying the Enemy & destroying their Works—Two Officers were killed & one wounded by a Bomb the Evening we opened—Lord Shuten's Cane was struck out of his Hand by a Cannon Ball—Lord Cornwallis has built a kind of Grotto at the foot of the secretary's Garden where he lives under Ground—A negroe of the Secretary's was kill'd in his House—It seems to be his Opinion that the British are a good deal dispirited altho' he says they affect to say they have no Apprehendsions of the Garrison's falling—An immense number of Negroes have died, in the most miserable Manner in York. . . .

Fryday 12th. Last night our second parallel was begun—It is within two hundred yards in some points of the Enemies Works—During the Course of this Day the Enemy have kept up a more considerable Fire than for some Days past, chiefly shells—they have kill'd & wounded five or six Men to day—A pretty constant Cannonade & Bombardment has been kept up from our Batteries during the Day & the last night—I have not yet been in the new Trenches and am not inform'd what new works we are erecting on our second Line.

Saturday 13th. The works on our second parallel were carried on last night with great Spirit. We lost some Men from the Enemies Fire which was rather encreased than diminish'd during the Night. The Enemy have drawn off most of their Ships across the Channel to the Gloster Shore—

St. George Tucker, journal entry about the Siege of Yorktown, 1781.

Surrender

As the siege of Yorktown wore on, General Charles Cornwallis understood the dire predicament of his army. Cut off from all supplies, his food stores ran low. Disease and casualties took their toll on his men. After the first week of October 1781, he had but 3,250 soldiers fit for duty—less than half of his command. On October 10 Cornwallis wrote to Sir Henry Clinton to communicate his dire circumstances. Suffering bombardments day and night from French and American cannon, he stressed his concern that his army could not hold out for long. Clinton responded that he would try to stage a rescue, but the effort was never made. On October 14 the American and French forces captured the last two defensive redoubts—or fortified positions— that guarded Yorktown. Further resistance was futile.

General Cornwallis's army surrenders to the American and French armies.

On October 16 Cornwallis tried unsuccessfully to evacuate his troops across a river. With his last plan dashed, he sent officers out the following day to discuss terms for surrendering his army. Two days later, on October 19, the British and Hessian troops under Cornwallis's command marched out of Yorktown, down a path flanked on one side by the smartly attired French army and on the other side by the ragtag colonial forces. Cornwallis sent word that he was too ill to attend the surrender ceremonies. He sent a subordinate to relinquish his sword to the victors. The British officer first tried to hand Cornwallis's sword to the Comte de Rochambeau, the French general, who politely directed the man to George Washington. Washington had General Benjamin Lincoln take the sword, as Lincoln had been forced to surrender his army to General Clinton at Charleston, South Carolina, under similar circumstances.

On October 20 Cornwallis wrote the following report to Clinton summarizing the events of the battle that made his surrender inevitable.

I have the mortification to inform your Excellency that I have been forced to give up the Posts of York and Gloucester, and to surrender the troops under my command, by capitulation, on the 19th instant, as prisoners of war to the combined forces of America and France.

I never saw this post in a very favorable light, but when I found I was to be attacked in it in so unprepared a state, by so powerful an army and artillery, nothing but the hopes of relief would have induced me to attempt its defense, for I would either have endeavored to escape to New York by rapid marches from the Gloucester side, immediately on the arrival of General Washington's troops at Williamsburg, or I would, notwithstanding the disparity of numbers, have attacked them in the open field, where it might have been just possible that fortune would have favored the gallantry of the handful of troops under my command, but being assured by your Excellency's letters that every possible means would be tried by the navy and army to relieve us, I could not think myself at liberty to venture upon either of those desperate attempts; therefore, after remaining for two days in a strong position in front of this place in hopes of being attacked, upon observing that the enemy were taking measures which could not fail of turning my left flank in a short time, and receiving on the second evening your letter of the 24th of September, informing me that the relief would sail about the 5th of October, I withdrew within the works on the night of the 29th of September, hoping by the labor and firmness of the soldiers to protract the defense until you could arrive. Everything was to be expected from the spirit of the troops, but every disadvantage attended their labor, as the works were to be continued under the enemy's fire, and our stock of intrenching tools, which did not much exceed 400 when we began to work in the latter end of August, was now much diminished. . . .

On the evening of the 14th [the colonial and French forces] assaulted and carried two redoubts that had been advanced about 300 yards for the purpose of delaying their approaches, and covering our left flank, and during the night included them in their second parallel [trench], on which they continued to work with the utmost exertion. Being perfectly sensible that our works could not stand many hours after the opening of the batteries of that parallel, we not only continued a constant fire with all our mortars and every gun that could be brought to bear upon it, but a little before daybreak on the morning of the 16th, I ordered a sortie of about 350 men, under the direction of Lieut.-Colonel Abercrombie, to attack two batteries which appeared to be in the greatest forwardness, and to spike the guns [make them unusable]. A detachment of Guards with the 80th company of Grenadiers, under the command of Lieut.-Colonel Lake, attacked the one, and one of light infantry, under the command of Major Armstrong, attacked the other, and both succeeded in forcing the redoubts that covered them, spiking 11 guns, and killing or wounding about 100 of the French troops, who had the guard of that part of the trenches, and with little loss on our side.

This action, though extremely honorable to the officers and soldiers who executed it, proved of little public advantage, for the cannon having been spiked in a hurry, were soon rendered fit for service again, and before dark the whole parallel and batteries appeared to be nearly complete. At this time we knew that there was no part of the whole front attacked on which we could show a single gun, and our shells were nearly expended. I, therefore, had only to choose between preparing to surrender next day, or endeavoring to get off with the greatest part of the troops, and I determined to attempt the latter. . . .

In this situation, with my little force divided, the enemy's batteries opened at daybreak. The passage between this place and Gloucester was much exposed, but the boats having now returned, they were ordered to bring back the troops that had passed during the night [in the effort to escape across the river], and they joined us in the forenoon without much loss. . . .

Our numbers had been diminished by the enemy's fire, but particularly by sickness, and the strength and spirits of those in the works were much exhausted, by the fatigue of constant watching and unremitting duty. Under all these circumstances, I thought it would have been wanton and inhuman to the last degree to sacrifice the lives of this small body of gallant soldiers, who had ever behaved with so much fidelity and courage, by exposing them to an assault which, from the numbers and precautions of the enemy, could not fail to succeed. I therefore proposed to capitulate; and I have the honor to enclose to your Excellency the copy of the correspondence between General Washington and me on that subject, and the terms of capitulation agreed upon. I sincerely lament that better could not be obtained, but I have neglected nothing in my power to alleviate the misfortune and distress of both officers and soldiers. The men are well clothed and provided with necessaries, and I trust will be regularly supplied by the means of the officers that are permitted to remain with them.

The treatment, in general, that we have received from the enemy since our surrender has been perfectly good and proper, but the kindness and attention that has been shown to us by the French officers in particular—their delicate sensibility of our situation—their generous and pressing offer of money, both public and private, to any amount—has really gone beyond what I can possibly describe, and will, I hope, make an impression on the breast of every British officer, whenever the fortune of war should put any of them into our power.

Charles Cornwallis, report to Sir Henry Clinton on the Battle of Yorktown, October 20, 1781.

A Reduction in the British Army Is Most Happily Effected

After the terms of surrender were signed on October 19, 1781, George Washington wrote this report to the Continental Congress apprising the members of the great victory at Yorktown. Washington's words reveal his characteristically reserved manner, as he is careful to convey his indebtedness to the French for their invaluable help in "reducing" the British army. After all, the victory at Yorktown did not immediately end the war, and Washington expected many battles

George Washington was grateful for France's contribution to the victory at Yorktown.

were yet to be fought before independence would be won. He had no way of knowing that the defeat of General Cornwallis's forces would bring about the fall of the English government and, in two years, the end of the war.

I have the honor to inform Congress that a reduction of the British army, under the command of Lord Cornwallis, is most happily effected. The unremitted ardor, which actuated every officer and soldier in the combined army on this occasion, has principally led to this important event at an earlier period than my most sanguine hopes had induced me to expect.

The singular spirit of emulation, which animated the whole army from the first commencement of our operations, has filled my mind with the highest pleasure and satisfaction, and had given me the happiest presages of success.

On the 17th instant, a letter was received from Lord Cornwallis, proposing a meeting of commissioners to consult on terms for the surrender of the posts of York and Gloucester. This letter (the first which had passed between us) opened a correspondence, a copy of which I do myself the honor to enclose; that correspondence was followed by the definitive capitulation, which was agreed to and signed on the 19th, a copy of which is also herewith transmitted and which, I hope, will meet the approbation of Congress.

I should be wanting in the feelings of gratitude, did I not mention on this occasion, with the warmest sense of acknowledgment, the very cheerful and able assistance which I have received in the course of our operation from his Excellency the Count de Rochambeau and all his officers of every rank in their respective capacities. Nothing could equal the zeal of our allies, but the emulating spirit of the American officers, whose ardor would not suffer their exertions to be exceeded.

The very uncommon degree of duty and fatigue, which the nature of the service required from the officers and engineers and artillery of both armies, obliges me particularly to mention the obligations I am under to the commanding and other officers of those corps. I wish it was in my power to express to Congress how much I feel myself indebted to the Count de Grasse and the officers of the fleet under his command, for the distinguished aid and support which has been afforded by them, between whom and the army the most happy concurrence of sentiments and views has subsisted, and from whom every possible cooperation has been experienced, which the most harmonious intercourse could afford.

George Washington, Report to Continental Congress on the Yorktown Surrender, October 19, 1781, in John C. Fitzpatrick, ed., *The Writings of George Washington, from the Original Manuscript Sources, 1745–1799.* 39 vols. Washington, D.C.: United States Government Printing Office, 1931–1944.

Parliament Debates the Surrender

The news of General Charles Cornwallis's surrender deeply divided Britain's Parliament. There was an immediate call for an investigation of Cornwallis's conduct. After a short examination of the matter, the duke of Chandos cleared all officers of any suspected negligence. Without Cornwallis as a scapegoat, the various members began assigning the blame to various ministers and factions within Parliament. The account of the parliamentary debates given below reveals that the duke of Chandos foisted the blame upon the earl of Sandwich, the first lord of the

Admiralty, for not having had the British fleet better used in support of Cornwallis's army.

Eventually in 1782 the members—pressured by the English people and the mounting costs of the war—voted "no confidence" in the King's ministers, and Lord North and the other men whom George III had appointed to manage the war resigned from office. Britain sent ambas-

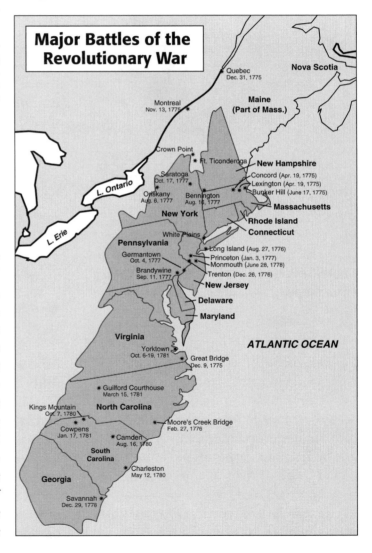

Major Battles of the Revolutionary War

Quebec Dec. 31, 1775

Nova Scotia

Montreal Nov. 13, 1775

Maine (Part of Mass.)

Crown Point

Ft. Ticonderoga

New Hampshire

Saratoga Oct. 17, 1777

Concord (Apr. 19, 1775)

Lexington (Apr. 19, 1775)

Bunker Hill (June 17, 1775)

L. Ontario

Oriskany Aug. 6, 1777

Bennington Aug. 16, 1777

New York

Massachusetts

Rhode Island

Connecticut

L. Erie

White Plains

Long Island (Aug. 27, 1776)

Pennsylvania

Germantown Oct. 4, 1777

Princeton (Jan. 3, 1777)

Monmouth (June 28, 1778)

Brandywine Sep. 11, 1777

Trenton (Dec. 26, 1776)

New Jersey

Delaware

Maryland

Virginia

Yorktown Oct. 6-19, 1781

ATLANTIC OCEAN

Great Bridge Dec. 9, 1775

Guilford Courthouse March 15, 1781

Kings Mountain Oct. 7, 1780

North Carolina

Moore's Creek Bridge Feb. 27, 1776

Cowpens Jan. 17, 1781

Camden Aug. 16, 1780

South Carolina

Charleston May 12, 1780

Georgia

Savannah Dec. 29, 1778

sadors to America to negotiate a cease-fire in November. There were some small skirmishes that took place after the armistice was signed, but no major battles. Final peace talks dragged on until 1783. On September 3 of that year, Britain and America signed the Treaty of Paris, officially ending the war and acknowledging the independence of the thirteen colonies.

March 6. The House having resolved itself into the said Committee, and the various papers moved for having been read,

The Duke of Chandos rose and observed, it was obvious, from the papers, that the officers stood fully acquitted of all blame. I find, he said, they have acted their parts, with fidelity to their country, though their services have been accompanied with disaster and disgrace: it is not therefore to their misconduct, that I am to attribute our present forlorn prospects; they have discharged their duty with an integrity becoming their characters; but, unfortunately, they were mortals, and could not resist those complicated difficulties, to which, by the misconduct of those at a distance, they were unhappily exposed. From the papers which have, day after day, been read to your lordships, nothing appears to me in a stronger light, than the immediate cause of the capture of the British army under lord Cornwallis, arose from the want of a sufficient force, to cover and protect it, in the Chesapeak: this is the ground upon which I place my foot; it is here, my lords, that I erect my standard. Owing to causes of a similar nature, owing to our

army being supplied with scanty handfuls of men, by which the superiority of the enemy, in point of numbers, has been supported and maintained, our misfortunes have accumulated upon us. This truth, I am confident, appears every where, from the history both of our naval and military operations in the western world. Had the army under lord Cornwallis been protected and supported by a powerful fleet in the Chesapeak, might it not have been saved from ruin, and the disgrace of its capture avoided? In like manner had sir H. Clinton been supplied with a proper number of troops, essential aid might have been communicated to lord Cornwallis, and his hands strengthened against the common enemy.

In applying this general observation to the present case, he did not, however, mean to throw the whole blame upon the Admiralty, for not having appointed a sufficient naval force to protect the British army at York-town. It was not novel doctrine, that they derived their authority, and received their orders, from the cabinet. Though they were responsible in some measure for their conduct, yet it was the cabinet that was ultimately amenable in the present instance. He meant, therefore, to direct the motions he was about to make against this collective body. It was owing to them that the army at York-town, under lord Cornwallis, had been captured, and America lost to this country. Why was not a greater number of ships sent upon so important a service? Where were the fleets of England now stationed? Why were not the armies of this country properly increased? Why did we not make alliances and confederacies with other countries, instead of sending half a dozen or a dozen British officers, all over Germany, to collect 1,000 or 1,500 mercenary troops, like so many poulterers employed in picking up as many chicken? Our disasters, continued the noble duke, press the present subject of enquiry upon my mind. . . .

His lordship concluded with observing, that though he was incapable of bringing any one over to his opinion, by his oratorical abilities, not being much practised in the habits of public speaking, yet he was convinced of the integrity of his own intentions, and of the justice of what he had advanced; he was, at all hazards, determined to pursue the conduct of that cabinet, which had brought disgrace upon the country, till at last the inflictions of justice were put in execution upon it. . . .

The Earl of Sandwich said, that he felt his task to be a very arduous one: that defending the plans of ministers, after those plans had unfortunately failed, was an extreme difficult matter to attempt; and however fair the intentions of ministers might have been, however wise their plans, as far as the situation of affairs, and the probable turn they would take, might appear to them at the time they formed these plans, it was by no means easy to combat the strong prejudices arising from ill success, or to convince men, whose minds were deeply impressed with senti-

ments of disappointment and mortification, that a calamity, which was certainly a very serious one, had been an instance of the uncertain chance of war, rather than a circumstance arising from neglect in ministers, from their want of foresight, or their want of caution. He most heartily agreed with the noble duke, and he was much pleased to find a mode of reasoning adopted by his grace, so exactly corresponding with his own sentiments for what was the language held by the noble duke, but that neither the first lord of the Admiralty, nor those connected with him in that department, were at all responsible for their conduct in that degree which might be commonly imagined. There was a trust reposed in them by the majority which decided in his Majesty's councils; and in proportion as they executed this charge with fidelity, they were justifiable or blameable. So much he would say; in concurrence with the noble duke, in behalf of himself, and in defence of those conjoined with him in office. He did not, however, mean, by this observation, to avoid saying any thing upon the present subject of debate, in answer to what had been stated by his grace. He had made an observation, and founded his motion upon it, that there was not a sufficient force to protect the army under lord Cornwallis at York-town. . . . He was convinced that any fault, or any neglect of duty, was not to be laid to [the Admiralty's] charge. He was equally well persuaded, that upon a due investigation of the matter, their lordships would find that the causes of the misfortune which formed the subject of the present enquiry, were to be attributed solely to accident, and not to those circumstances which had been suggested by the noble duke. He would, therefore, state to them the precise facts respecting the situation and numbers of the British fleet in the West Indies and America, at the time alluded to; from which it would appear, that the lords of the Admiralty proceeded upon solid presumptions in their administration, and that neither they, nor those who in the aggregate directed his Majesty's councils, were at all criminal on the occasion. . . . The noble duke had asked, where were the fleets and armies of England? He would tell him, some of them were in America; many of them in the West and East Indies; and not a few employed at home. In short the Admiralty had arranged matters agreeably to the best of their judgment; and he would add, without dreading being taxed with presumption, to the best of their abilities. We had been unfortunate, it was true. The minds of mankind were of course affected; their prejudices awakened; and they were consequently led to enquire after, and conjure up causes, which, in fact, had no existence. Our misfortunes originated in an unhappy combination of circumstances, and the hand of Providence did not seem to favour us. These were the real sources of our disasters, and it was in vain to seek for them elsewhere.

Britain's Parliament, Debates Over the Surrender of Cornwallis, March 6, 1782.

A Loyalist Remains Defiant

Although the armistice of 1782 ended the fighting between Crown forces and the colonials, the feuding in the backcountry of the Carolinas between Tories—loyalists who sympathized with England—and Whigs—colonials who favored independence—did not cease. Indeed, news of Parliament's decision to work toward a peace left many loyalists feeling betrayed. Without British protection, they could only expect increased harassment from their Whig neighbors. Many Tories even feared they would be hunted down and murdered for their loyalty to the Crown.

In a March 31 letter to a friend in England, John Hamilton, a loyalist from South Carolina, expresses astonishment that England would give up the struggle and abandon those who had so faithfully served the king's cause. Hamilton hopes in vain that Parliament will change its mind and that the war will continue. In fact, after the Treaty of Paris in 1783, sporadic feuds between former Tories and Whigs did flare up in many southern colonies, a sign that the nation had achieved independence but that the people had not yet become united.

I was in a State of Despondence for some time untill his Majesty's speech arrived when it revived my Spirits, but what was my astonishment when I Read Lord George G[ermai]n's and Lord North's speech in parliament; surely they can never be so weak as to give up this Country.

Our Country is lost in dissipation, luxury and faction. There is no publick

Spirit or virtue left either to reward merit or punish offences. Remove all Such wretches from power and leav either Execution of affairs to the brave, zealous Loyalists, who have lost their fortunes and Risk'd their lives in defence of their King and Country; such are the men who will save their Country from Ruin and distruction. . .

Notwithstanding all our Misfortunes, Great Britain can never, must never relinquish America. The last man and shilling must be expended before she gives America her independence; if she looses America, she looses all her West Indies and must Revert again to her insular Situation, which hardly make her visible on the face of the Earth.

Some examples must be made. A General, an Admiral and others must pay for our Misfortunes; a Spirited minister must take place and an honest man who will reward merit and punish the offenders. Then we may Expect to become ourselves again, but not before a very great change is made.

I still flatter myself the war will be carried on with vigour in North Carolina and Virginia and a large reinforcement sent out this season. The inhabitants are tired of their French Connections and with the Tyranny of their Leaders which is more conspicuous than ever. It behoves the nation at large to interfere and prevent the Ministry from giving America her independence. Your Salvation depends on Spirited Exertions at present, if not and America is given up, Britain must become a Province of France and America.

John Hamilton, letter regarding the treatment of loyalists, March 31, 1782.

✬ Chronology of Events ✬

1763

The French and Indian War (fought between England and France in North America) ends.

1765

King George III of England approves the Stamp Act, which taxes the American colonies in order to cover part of the expense of the French and Indian War; colonists protest the tax as unfair because it was levied without colonial representation in Parliament.

1766

Parliament repeals the Stamp Act but asserts its right to tax the colonies through the newly drafted Declaratory Act.

1767

English financial adviser Charles Townshend devises a new set of taxes for the colonies; the Townshend Acts are met with more protest.

1768

Boston firebrand Samuel Adams calls for a boycott of English imports; in response, England sends troops to the colonies to maintain order.

1770

In March five colonists are killed after a brief confrontation with British soldiers outside Boston's customs house; the Boston Massacre adds to the tensions in the colonies; Parliament repeals most of the Townshend Acts.

1773

Parliament tries to save the East India Company by pushing its tea on the colonies; however, to gain revenue, Parliament passes the Tea Act, which adds a hidden tax to the East India tea; the colonists are not deceived; in December a band of angry colonists board East India ships in Boston harbor and dump the cargo of tea into the harbor; the Boston Tea Party is considered an act of rebellion by King George III.

1774

Parliament punishes Boston for the Tea Party by closing the city's port and passing other regulations collectively known as the Intolerable Acts; to keep the peace, British general Thomas Gage is made governor of Massachusetts; in September the colonies send delegates to the First Continental Congress to address the tensions between England and America.

1775

General Gage is given permission to repress rebellion in the colonies; he sends units to nearby Lexington and Concord to seize colonial munitions; the colonists are alerted to his move, and militia units from neighboring colonies converge on Concord to stop the British advance; the two sides exchange fire and the British are forced to retreat to Boston; the Continental Congress meets again to discuss breaking free from English rule; it appoints George Washington as the commander of military forces in America; before Washington can arrive to take charge of the patriot units around Boston, British troops strike and achieve what is for them a very costly victory at the Battle of Bunker Hill; in August, after finally hearing of the skirmish at Lexington and Concord, King George III declares the colonies to be in rebellion.

1776

In January, Thomas Paine argues for colonial independence in his influential and widely circulated pamphlet entitled *Common Sense;* in March the British evacuate Boston, which is now under siege by Washington's army; in July the Continental Congress votes to declare American independence; it adopts Thomas Jefferson's Declaration of Independence as its testimonial of British abuses and American resolve to be free; in August, British general William Howe invades and captures New York; Washington's patriot army is chased back to Pennsylvania; in December, Washington stages a daring surprise attack on Trenton, New Jersey, where Hessian mercenaries working for the British have camped for the winter; the attack is successful and bolsters Washington's reputation and patriot morale.

1777

The colonial armies are defeated at Brandywine and Germantown in Pennsylvania; the British enter Philadelphia, the seat of the colonial government; while Washington fights his delaying actions, colonial general Horatio Gates achieves a resounding victory over British general John Burgoyne's army near Saratoga, New York; Burgoyne's army is the first British command to surrender to patriot forces; the victory prompts French king Louis XVI to recognize American independence.

1778

In February, Benjamin Franklin helps broker a formal military alliance between France and America; William Howe resigns his post as commander of British forces in America; in June, Henry Clinton becomes Howe's successor and pulls all British forces in the northern colonies back to New York; in July, France declares war on England.

1779

Spain officially declares war on Great Britain.

1780

Clinton sails from New York to South Carolina with a part of his army; there, he captures Charleston and leaves Charles Cornwallis in the South to control the region; Clinton returns to New York.

1781

Lord Cornwallis, by his own initiative, begins a fruitless rampage through the Carolinas and into Virginia chasing elusive colonial troops; Clinton orders Cornwallis to cease his activities and camp by the Virginia coast, where he can be ready to support Clinton in a New England campaign; Cornwallis reluctantly obeys and stations his army at Yorktown; French troops arrive in Rhode Island; their commander, the Comte de Rochambeau, persuades General Washington to stage an offensive in the South against Cornwallis; with the French fleet cutting off Cornwallis's retreat by sea, the combined American and French armies surround Yorktown and force Cornwallis to surrender on October 19; the British public turns against continuing the war; the wartime government falls, and Parliament seeks peace with the colonies.

1782

British and French representatives agree to a treaty in Paris, France.

1783

The Treaty of Paris is signed in September and the war ends, despite the fact that the Continental Congress would not finish ratifying the treaty until the following year; in November, George Washington resigns his commission as head of the Continental army.

☆ Index ☆

Adams, Abigail, 61–62
Adams, John, 54, 55, 61–62
Adams, Samuel
  Boston Tea Party and, 18
  boycotts and, 9
  on independence, 72–73
  Lexington and Concord (battles) and, 30, 33
  on Townshend Acts, 8, 15
Allen, Ethan (colonel), 42–44
American Revolution
  causes of, 7–29
  early battles of, 30–52
  final campaigns and events of, 99–118
  major campaigns of, 74–98
  military strategies of, 74
  purpose of, 53–73
Americans, 90
American unity, 56, 57
army
  American, 32, 89–90
  British, 89–90
  see also Hessians; militia; minutemen
Arnold, Benedict, 42, 43, 92–93

Bangs, Isaac, 66–68
Barrett, Amos, 39
bayonets, 46, 89–90
Bernard, Francis, 12–14
Bill of Rights, 57
Bonhomme Richard (ship), 103–106
Boston Gazette (newspaper), 18
Boston Massacre, 15–17
Boston Tea Party, 17–21
boycotts
  First Continental Congress on, 22–23, 24
  Townshend Acts reaction, 9, 15
  Virginia House of Burgesses support of, 23
Brant, Joseph, 77–80
Breed's Hill. See Bunker Hill
Bunker Hill (battle), 45–49
Burgoyne, John (general), 31, 45, 77, 92–94

Canada, 60
Carleton, Guy (general), 101

cease-fire, 101
Clinton, Henry (general)
  Boston battles and, 31, 45
  final command to Cornwallis, 107
  Long Island (battle) and, 81
  Rhode Island capture and, 75
  southern strategy of, 100
  succession to supreme commander of English troops, 99
Common Sense (Paine), 55–57
Concord (battle), 30, 32–40
Concord Bridge, 39–40
Continental Congress. See First Continental Congress; Second Continental Congress
Cornwallis, Charles (general)
  Brandywine battle and, 84–85
  Charleston occupation and, 100
  Parliamentary debate of conduct of, 114–17

Virginia campaigns of, 100
Yorktown (battle) and, 107–108, 109–12

Dawes, William, 33–36
Declaration of Colonial Rights and Grievances, 24–27
Declaration of Independence
adoption of, 55
New York reaction to, 66–68
Second Continental Congress and, 61–63
text of, 63–66
writing of, 53–55
Declaratory Act of 1766, 8, 14–15
Delaware River crossing, 75, 82–84

East India Company, 17–18, 96

Ferguson, James, 85
Ferguson, Patrick, 85
First Continental Congress
appointment of Washington as commander, 32
colonist grievances statement by, 24–27
instructions for Virginia delegates to, 21–24
petition of grievances and, 10
purpose of, 53

Fort Ticonderoga (battle), 42–44
France
aid to American cause, 77, 99, 102–103
American discussion of role of, 60, 61
American requests for assistance from, 75–77
arguments against alliance with, 106–107
Saratoga victory effect on, 93
Franklin, Benjamin, 63, 99, 102–103
French and Indian Wars, 7–8

Gage, Thomas (general)
Boston battles and, 31–32, 45
Boston fortification and, 9, 21, 23
Lexington and Concord (battles) and, 32–33, 38, 39
Gates, Horatio (general), 77, 92, 93
George III (king of England), 8, 41
Germantown raid, 86–88
Glover, John, 93
Grasse, François de (admiral), 100–101, 107, 114
Green Mountain Boys, 42–44
Greene, Nathanael (general), 86

grievances, 24–27
see also Declaration of Independence; rights

Hamilton, John, 117
Hancock, John, 17, 30, 33, 51
Henry, Patrick, 27–29
Hessians
detention of, in Boston, 94–97
French alliance and, 61
Long Island (battle) and, 80, 82
Trenton (battle) and, 75, 83
House of Burgesses. See Virginia House of Burgesses
Howe, William (general)
Boston battles and, 31–32
Bunker Hill battle and, 45, 46, 48–49
New York campaigns and, 74–75, 80–82
resignation of, 99
strategies for war, 74, 84
Hulton, Anne, 19–21
Hutchinson, Thomas, 68

independence
arguments against, 68–71, 90, 117–18
arguments for, 55–57, 61–62, 63–66, 72–73
Declaration of Independence, 53–55
Intolerable Acts, 9–10

Jefferson, Thomas, 53–55
Jones, John Paul (naval captain), 103–106

Lafayette, Marie-Joseph de (general), 76–77, 88, 107
Lee, Richard Henry, 53
Lexington (battle), 30–31, 33, 36–39, 40
Lincoln, Benjamin (general), 100, 110
Longfellow, Henry Wadsworth, 30
Long Island (battle), 80–82
loyalists, 19–21, 68–71, 90–92, 117–18

Mason, George, 57
Massachusetts Spy (newspaper), 37
McKenzie, Frederick, 40
mercenaries. *See* Hessians
militia, 45–48
minutemen, 39–40
Mohawk, 77–80
muskets, 85

Narrative of Colonel Ethan Allen's Captivity (Allen), 43
Native Americans, 77–80
navy
  American, 103–106
  British, 18, 45, 103–106
  French, 99, 100, 107

New York Loyal Gazette (newspaper), 90
North Bridge, 36–37, 39–40

Otis, James, 10–11

Paine, Thomas, 55–56
Parliament
  acts of, 7, 8, 9, 14–15
  American grievances against, 10–11, 21–26
  statements from, 114–17
patriots. *See* Americans
Preston, Thomas, 15–17
prisoners of war, 94–97
Putnam, Israel (general), 45, 46, 47, 80

Quartering Act, 9

Revenue Act, 11
Revere, Paul, 32, 33–36
Riedesel, Frederika von, 94–97
rifles, 85
rights, 11, 22, 25–26, 55, 57–59.
  see also Declaration of Independence; grievances
Rights of the British Colonies Asserted and Proved (Otis), 10
Rivington, James, 90–92
Rochambeau, Jean-Baptiste de (general), 100, 101, 110

Saratoga (battle), 77, 92–94
Second Continental Congress, 53, 59–62
Serapis (ship), 103–106
Shaw, Samuel, 106–107
slavery, 55
Sons of Liberty, 9, 33
Spain
  aid to Americans, 77
  alliance with France, 102
  role of, discussed by Second Continental Congress, 60, 61
  Saratoga victory effect on, 93
spies. *See* Sons of Liberty
Stamp Act, 8, 11–14
Strictures upon the Declaration of the Congress at Philadelphia (Hutchinson), 68
Sugar Act, 11
Sullivan, John, 86
surrender (British), 101, 109–12

taxation, 8–9, 11–14
  see also grievances; Parliament; rights
Tories. *See* loyalists
Townshend Acts, 8, 15, 17–18
trade, 7
Treaty of Paris, 101
Tucker, St. George, 108
Tudor, John, 15–17

Valley Forge, 97–98
Virginia Declaration of Rights, 57–59
Virginia Gazette (newspaper), 87
Virginia House of Burgesses, 21–24, 27–29

Waldo, Albigence, 98
Warren, Joseph, 45, 46, 47
Washington, George (general)
appointment to command patriot army, 49–50
Boston victory and, 51–52
Brandywine (battle) and, 84–85
defeat in New York, 75
Delaware River crossing and, 75
siege of Boston and, 32
strategies for war, 74
tactical and leadership abilities of, 75–76
Yorktown victory report of, 112–14
Washington, Martha, 49
Whigs. *See* Americans
Wirt, William, 27

Yorktown (campaign), 100–101, 108–109, 110–12

⭐ Picture Credits ⭐

★ About the Editor ★

Author David M. Haugen edits books for Lucent Books and Greenhaven Press. He holds a master's degree in English literature and has also worked as a writer and instructor.